Before Nomination

Before Nomination
Our Primary Problems
edited by George Grassmuck

A conference sponsored by the Gerald R. Ford Foundation,
the American Enterprise Institute for Public Policy Research, and
The University of Michigan

American Enterprise Institute for Public Policy Research
Washington, D.C.

George Grassmuck is secretary of the Gerald R. Ford Foundation and professor of political science at The University of Michigan.

This conference on presidential primaries was held at the Gerald R. Ford Library, April 24–26, 1985.

Library of Congress Cataloging-in-Publication Data
Main entry under title:

Before nomination.
  Includes index.
  1. Presidents—United States—Nomination—Addresses, essays, lectures.
  2. Primaries—United States—Addresses, essays, lectures. I. Title.
  JK522.B44 1985   324.5′4   85-22850
  ISBN 0-8447-2260-X
  ISBN 0-8447-2259-6 (pbk)

  1 3 5 7 9 10 8 6 4 2

  AEI Symposia 85E

ON THE COVER, LEFT TO RIGHT: Frank J. Fahrenkopf, Gerald R. Ford, and Paul Kirk

Printed in the United States of America

To Bob Griffin
Chairman of the Board, Gerald R. Ford Foundation,
1981–1985

Contents

PART THREE
SUMMARY, COLLOQUY, AND RECOMMENDATIONS

Preface

George Grassmuck

Every conference worth the name is an adventure. From idea to event, plans, patterns, and issues are carefully controlled. Then the arguments, the responses, and the conclusions run their own course. This compilation carries these presentations and discussions as it echoes the tones of the event, its harmonies and its dissonances.

Responding to President Ford's challenge, the researched articles presented by academic participants take up the center pages. These authors had an opportunity after the conference to revise their contributions. The discussants were not so fortunate.

The last part of the book carries the rapporteur's synthesis, the essence of exchanges by those experienced in politics, and the summaries of group reports and recommendations presented at the end of the conference. Tapes and a court reporter's transcript served as the record from which the exchanges, reports, and recommendations were drawn.

Karl Palachuk has been my editorial assistant. I am indebted to him, to James D. Shortt, assistant to the president of The University of Michigan, and to the office staff of the Department of Political Science at the university for their aid, encouragement, and patience. The President's Fund at the university supported the editing.

Marvin L. Esch, director of seminars and programs, and other members of the American Enterprise Institute for Public Policy Research gave advice and guidance that were much needed and willingly offered.

A condensed report of this conference in a single, economic volume must entail reordering, reductions in commentary, and elisions. The liberties that have been taken, as well as any omissions or inaccuracies, remain my responsibility.

Participants

DAVID W. ADAMANY is president of Wayne State University. A lawyer and political scientist, he has held administrative posts in Wisconsin state government, including the position of chairman of the State Elections Board. He is the author of *Campaign Finance in America* and coauthor of *Political Money*.

HERBERT E. ALEXANDER is professor of political science at the University of Southern California and director of the Citizens Research Foundation, which specializes in campaign finance analysis. The most recent of his many publications on campaign finance are *Financing the 1980 Election* and the third edition of *Financing Politics*.

PHILIP W. BUCHEN, a trustee of the Gerald R. Ford Foundation, is a partner in the Washington law firm of Dewey, Ballantine, Busby, Palmer and Wood. In 1941 Philip Buchen's law partner was Gerald Ford. During the Ford administration Buchen served as counsel to the president.

RICHARD CHENEY is United States representative at large from Wyoming. He served as chief of staff of the Ford White House. He and his wife, Lynne, are the authors of *Kings of the Hill: Power and Personality in the House of Representatives*.

PHILIP CONVERSE is a past president of the American Political Science Association. He is Robert Angell Distinguished Professor of Sociology and Political Science at The University of Michigan and since 1982 has been director of the Center for Political Studies of the Institute for Social Research there.

FRANK J. FAHRENKOPF, a Reno attorney, was unanimously elected to a two-year term as chairman of the Republican National Committee in January 1983. Before his election as chairman, he headed the Nevada Republican party.

ROBERT H. FINCH practices law in California. He has held numerous offices in state government there, including lieutenant governor and chairman of the California State Senate. During the Nixon administration, Finch was secretary and counselor to the president.

MARLIN FITZWATER, a career federal employee, held press relations posts at the Treasury and Transportation departments and the Environmental Protection Agency before going to the White House as deputy press secretary. He is now press secretary to Vice President George Bush.

GERALD R. FORD has been United States representative from Michigan (1949–1973), minority leader of the House (1965–1973), vice president (1973–1974) and thirty-eighth president of the United States (1974–1977). His memoir, *A Time to Heal*, was published in 1979.

GEORGE GRASSMUCK is secretary of the Gerald R. Ford Foundation and professor of political science at The University of Michigan. He was chief of research for the 1960 Republican presidential campaign and served as special assistant to the secretary of health, education, and welfare and as executive assistant in the Nixon White House.

ALEXANDER HEARD, after serving for twenty years as chancellor of Vanderbilt University, has resumed his duties as professor of political science and accepted responsibility for a long-term study of the presidential selection process. He has written extensively on the American political system.

HAMILTON JORDAN was chief political adviser and chief of staff to President Jimmy Carter. He has been a political commentator for Cable News Network in Atlanta since 1981.

XANDRA KAYDEN, a Ph.D. graduate of Harvard, has taught at the University of Massachusetts. She is a consultant and a member of the Campaign Finance Study Group, which is associated with Harvard's Institute of Politics. Her publications include *Campaign Organization* and the forthcoming *The Party Goes On*.

PAUL KIRK was elected chairman of the Democratic National Committee on February 1, 1985. Most recently a partner in a Worcester, Massachusetts, law office, Kirk was special assistant to Senator Edward M. Kennedy from 1971 to 1977.

THEODORE J. LOWI received his M.A. and Ph.D. degrees from Yale University. He taught at the University of Chicago before becoming the John L. Senior Professor of American Institutions at Cornell. His many publications include *The End of Liberalism* and, most recently, *The Personal President*.

MICHAEL J. MALBIN is a resident fellow at the American Enterprise Institute, a contributing editor to the *National Journal*, and an adjunct professor at Catholic University. His books include *Religion and Politics; Unelected Representatives: The New Role of Congressional Staff;* and *Money and Politics in the United States*.

CHARLES T. MANATT of California has held a number of leadership positions in Democratic state and national organizations, including chairman of the Democratic National Committee. He is a member of the Washington law firm of Manatt, Phelps, Rothenberg, and Tunney.

THOMAS E. MANN has been executive director of the American Political Science Association since 1981. Adjunct scholar at the American Enterprise Institute, he wrote *Unsafe at Any Margin: Interpreting Congressional Elections* and was coauthor of *Vital Statistics on Congress*.

DAVID MATHEWS, a former president of the University of Alabama, was secretary of health, education, and welfare in President Gerald Ford's administration. He is chief executive officer of the Charles F. Kettering Foundation in Dayton, Ohio.

WARREN E. MILLER, a past president of the American Political Science Association, is a professor of political science at Arizona State University and an adjunct professor of political science at The University of Michigan. He is associate director of the Inter-university Consortium for Political and Social Research and the author of books and articles on the voter and the national election process.

MICHAEL NELSON is associate professor of political science at Vanderbilt University. A former editor of *The Washington Monthly*, he has written widely on political subjects in numerous journals. He edited and contributed to *The Presidency and the Political System* (1984) and is coauthor of *Presidents, Politics, and Policy* (1984).

LANA POLLACK, Democratic state senator in Michigan, has been a campaign director many times and a city chairman for her party in Ann Arbor.

NELSON POLSBY is professor of political science at the University of California, Berkeley. He is the author of numerous books and articles on American and British politics. Among his publications are *Presidential Elections* (with Aaron Wildavsky, now in its sixth edition), *Congress and the Presidency*, and *Consequences of Party Reform*.

AUSTIN RANNEY is a resident scholar at the American Enterprise Institute. He has taught at the University of Illinois, the University of Wisconsin, and Georgetown University and is a former president of the American Political Science Association. *Channels of Power: The Impact of Television on American Politics* is his most recent book.

TERRY SANFORD, president of Duke University since 1969, was governor of North Carolina from 1961 to 1965. He is a trustee and member of numerous organizations concerned with education, government, and urban matters. *A Danger of Democracy* is the most recent of his three books.

WILLIAM SCHNEIDER is a resident fellow at the American Enterprise Institute. Before joining AEI, he was an associate professor of government at Harvard and a research fellow at the Hoover Institution. A columnist for the *Los Angeles Times* syndicate, his latest book, *The Confidence Gap: Business, Labor, and Government in the Public Mind*, was written with Seymour Lipset.

NEIL STAEBLER, a native of Ann Arbor, is a businessman and former member of Congress. He served as vice-chairman of the Twentieth Century Fund Task Force on Financing Congressional Campaigns and, from 1975 to 1978, was a member of the Federal Election Commission. He wrote *The Campaign Finance Revolution*.

ROBERT TEETER, executive vice-president of Market Opinion Research of Detroit, is head of the firm's political division, which provides polling and political advice to Republican candidates and organizations.

MICHAEL W. TRAUGOTT is adjunct professor of political science and senior study director at the Center for Political Studies, Institute for Social Research, The University of Michigan. He is a media consultant and coauthor of *Campaigning for Congress*.

WERNER VEIT was managing editor and editor of the *Grand Rapids Press* from 1963 to 1979. Since 1978 he has been president of the Booth Newspaper chain. He is on the Board of Trustees of the Gerald R. Ford Foundation.

JACK WALKER, professor of political science and public policy at The University of Michigan, has written books and articles on the presidency, including "The Presidency and the Nominating System," in Michael Nelson, ed., *The Presidency and the Political System.*

MARTIN P. WATTENBERG, who received his Ph.D. from The University of Michigan in 1982, teaches at the University of California, Irvine. His book *The Decline of American Political Parties, 1952–1980* was published by Harvard University Press in 1984.

DON W. WILSON is director of the Gerald R. Ford Library and Museum. Holder of a doctorate in American history, he is an adjunct lecturer in that discipline at The University of Michigan.

Before
Nomination

Part One
Purpose

Planning and Organizing

Don W. Wilson

Early in 1984 the Program Committee of the Gerald R. Ford Foundation recommended that a conference on the presidential nominating process be held at the Gerald R. Ford Library on the campus of The University of Michigan. President Ford enthusiastically accepted the idea, actively participated in the framing of the program, and suggested topics and participants.

The Program Committee, chaired by Philip W. Buchen, formulated the broad concept of the conference and based it on three primary goals: the conference should focus on the presidential primary process; it should include a balanced representation of scholars and political practitioners; and the results of its deliberations should receive wide public dissemination. An advisory group of political scientists—Philip Converse, George Grassmuck, Alexander Heard, Warren E. Miller, and Nelson Polsby—were called upon to help organize the program and suggest appropriate scholars to present the academic papers. Through the personal interest and involvement of President Ford, the foundation was able to attract leading practitioners and scholars from around the country.

Bipartisan in membership and exhibiting diverse opinions on the nature of reform, the conference raised as many questions as it proposed solutions. Both participants and observers, however, believed that progress had been made in understanding the complex issues involved in the presidential primary system.

These proceedings are the result of that detailed planning and a great deal of interinstitutional cooperation. Among the significant contributors were The University of Michigan, the Center for the Study of the Presidency at Vanderbilt University, and the American Enterprise Institute for Public Policy Research, the publishers of the proceedings. Without that broad cooperation and interest the quality of this conference and its deliberations would have been significantly diminished.

A substantial grant from the Gannett Foundation provided funds for the conference and this record.

The Challenge

Gerald R. Ford

It is my privilege to welcome you to this conference on presidential primaries and related activities that make up the way candidates vie for presidential nomination. I believe that the growing number of uncoordinated primaries, caucuses, and conventions needs careful and knowledgeable reexamination. I am grateful to the experienced political activists, select scholars, and established journalists who join me here for that purpose, and I look forward to their prepared statements and to the discussions and recommendations we have scheduled.

In the summer of 1940, as I was just about to complete my law courses at Yale, I joined the crowds outside the Republican convention hall and cheered in support of Wendell Willkie, who won nomination on the sixth ballot. Things have changed since then, as I found in my 1976 presidential campaign, and they have not improved in the last ten years. The endless succession of presidential primaries just bores voters. We have repeatedly revised the ways in which delegates to the national conventions are selected, still without interesting the national electorate, and we have passed campaign finance legislation with all good intentions but without achieving major improvement in the nominating process.

In 1984 we put candidates, the media, and party supporters through an exhausting exercise before the two major parties picked their nominees. The prenomination race ran through thirty-nine state caucuses, some Republican and some Democratic, fifty-two primaries of both parties, and a large number of state and local conventions. The preseason activity began long before, but the open season began in January 1984, when House and Senate Democrats met to select convention delegates from among their members. It ended on June 5, when primaries were held in seven states, border to border and coast to coast. National media covered the Iowa caucuses in February and gave them national significance. A week later the New Hampshire primaries became "first Tuesday." The press labeled March 13 "super Tuesday," with primaries in three southern and two New England states, and June 5 became "last Tuesday," when candidates were asked to meet the voters in New Jersey and California at the same time. Airport appearances with cameras at work became the necessity of the day as exhausted candidates shuttled across the continent.

The Federal Election Commission allowed each candidate a maximum of $24 million for efforts to win nomination. Yet, by the end of May, Gary Hart was over $4 million in debt and Walter Mondale over $3 million. John Glenn, out of the race, had a debt of $3 million, and Alan Cranston had about $1.5 million in obligations. Even with government financing, the cost of preconvention campaigns exceeds the resources of candidates and their supporters. Should candidates look to private sources for more funds? Must they anticipate the uncontrolled support of independent groups and committees as sources of their campaign strength? I question that, as I question the need for so many independent primaries and other campaign events. In my opinion their increased number defeats their fundamental purpose.

The purpose is to nominate the best, the most capable, and the most representative candidate that each of our two great parties can find. Our political democracy and our most talented leaders, in office and out, must not be hobbled by a growth of uncoordinated requirements, which themselves determine who shall be selected.

So let me challenge this distinguished group to consider these questions, among others, during the course of this conference:

• Does our present set of prenomination actions assure the parties of a choice between the best possible candidates?

• Can we spare candidates, voters, and the media some of the duress that is built into our present selection process?

• Are likely candidates who now hold office in Washington or in state capitals excluded or hampered by today's primaries and caucuses?

• Does the protection of sovereign states within our federal structure require that a candidate conform to state scheduling of campaign events?

I am most optimistic that the competence of this talented gathering will give full and fruitful consideration to these critical issues. They must be addressed and answered if our republican system of government is to remain effective in this large nation.

Thus I charge you to come up with a utopian answer. Now let me qualify that charge.

As a realist in politics all my life, one who thought we should always attempt what could be accomplished rather than what some extremists on either side recommended, I suggest to all of you that you try to find some realistic answers to the solution of the most apparent problem—that the public believes the process costs too much money and takes too much time. In searching for the realistic and not the utopian answer, there are some limits that I think have to be faced.

First is the constitutional issue of freedom of speech as it relates to the expenditure of funds. I do not foresee any change by the Supreme Court as to what a person may spend on his own behalf or what a so-called independent committee may spend. So we have to deal with that reality.

Second, I do not see any prospect for change in the Constitution itself, by the traditional amending process, that might change the way we nominate candidates.

Third, there is obviously a role for the political parties. Frank Fahrenkopf and Paul Kirk, as chairs respectively of the Republican and Democratic national committees, have a duty in the near future to see what the political parties can do to make the process of nominating candidates better. From what I have heard, Frank Fahrenkopf and Charles Manatt, then head of the Democratic National Committee, worked together on the 1984 process to the extent that such cooperation was feasible. I believe Frank and Paul will do the same as we move into the 1988 nominating process. This conference may conclude that some things can or should be done in this regard. So a charge to the heads of the two major political parties, as to what their role or responsibility might be, would be helpful.

Next, we must take into account the role of the states. Whether our group can come up with an answer that will change the positions of New Hampshire and Iowa is somewhat problematic, but it does appear to me that we should search for suggestions that might get those states and perhaps others to co-operate in an effort to condense the time span between the opening gun and the last salvo before the two major conventions. I see this as an area in which some specific recommendations might be fruitful.

Then there is a new aspect of the nominating process—the development of an industry. I am not critical of it, but I have seen at first hand the growing influence of an industry in the nominating process, of pollsters, advertisers, the whole range of candidate production. This is not an inconsequential operation in our society, and I do not know what should be done, if anything, to control or limit the extraordinary impact of that group on our nominating process. This large, active group ought to be examined from time to time, because it is costly and because each presidential election year sees expenditures increasing. The public gets a little suspicious at one point or another when the magnitude of expenditures is revealed.

After I look at the various limitations we face, I am more convinced than ever that we cannot come up with a utopian response. But it will be highly desirable if we can be seen as a group that took an honest look and came up with responsible solutions or proposals that generated more public support for, and more confidence in, the process of nominating the candidates for the presidency of the United States.

Our government works best when the people believe the process for choosing leaders is an honest, forthright, constructive way in which they participate in their government. So I charge you to do your best, and I look forward to your specific recommendations.

6

Part Two

Prepared Presentations

Constitution, Government, and Politics

Theodore J. Lowi

The United States Constitution had little to say about politics and nothing about political parties. The power to regulate elections was delegated almost entirely to the states (Article I, sections 2, 4). Presidential election itself was left to the states, except in instances to be noted below.

Most of the founders saw peril in politics. To them politics was a problem, for which the Constitution was a particular kind of solution. In probably the most famous of the *Federalist Papers*, No. 10, Madison recognized in his opening passages that popular governments have a propensity to develop the "dangerous vice" of faction and went on to support ratification of the Constitution as "a proper cure" for the "mischiefs of faction." Since prevention of faction would be a cure far worse than the disease, the only alternative was to foster the largest possible number of factions so that no single faction or conspiracy among factions could reach majority size and impose its will on all others. This made democracy of continental scale superior to smaller-scale democracies, and it made the legislature in a republic the superior form of government because the "temporary or partial considerations" of factions would be regulated by "passing them through the medium of a chosen body of citizens, whose wisdom . . . will be more consonant to the public good than if pronounced by the people themselves." Fear of political parties was particularly strong because party was understood to be a faction nearing majority size. Washington in his Farewell Address (the drafting of which was shared by Madison as well as Hamilton) warned of "the baneful effects of the spirit of party."

Yet the Constitution produced a distinctive form of politics, and as the Constitution changed, so did the politics. This relation between Constitution and politics is the best guide for tracing political development because, as a general rule, *every regime tends to produce a politics consonant with itself.* In other words, as people organize into factions and parties to control the government, the structure of that government will be the most important determinant of the shape of the politics.

Table 1 identifies three regimes in American history. Finer distinctions could be made and more regimes identified. But these will be sufficient. On

9

TABLE 1
U.S. REGIMES AND THEIR POLITICS

Regime	Politics
Regime of the founding, with parliamentary government (1789–c.1804)	Republicanism, or institutional democracy • Parliamentary parties • Nomination by electors
Regime of patronage, with congressional government (c.1804–c.1939)	Party democracy • Patronage parties • Nomination by party delegations in national convention
Regime of regulation and redistribution, with presidential government (c.1939–)	Mass democracy "Partisanship with parties," or "taxation parties"

the left is a brief characterization of the regime and its central feature of government. On the right is a characterization of the form of politics, particularly the method of presidential selection.

The Regime of the Founding

Although the regime of the founding lasted no more than twenty years, they wre among the most momentous years in the history of the Republic. These were precedent-making years, during which the government was required to make one-time-only policies: The major departments and the judiciary had to be established. Recognition as a nation-state had to be established. The domestic and international legitimacy of the national government had to be established by assuming all debts previously incurred by the national government and the states. The power of the national government to tax the citizens of the United States had to be established. This was a regime of state building.

The politics of the founding period took its shape around these issues. Political parties were emerging in Congress even as Washington was trying to mobilize Americans against them. Within three years of Washington's retirement, virtually 90 percent of the members of Congress were identified with one of the two emerging parties, and they voted with more party regularity than is seen in Congress today. Moreover, the differences between the two parties were much more policy oriented and ideological than those of the party systems of later epochs.[1]

The political parties of the founding period were parliamentary parties in a system that can be best understood as a modified parliamentary system. Under Article I, section 8, Congress possessed all the powers of the national government while program and leadership came from the executive. Secretary of the Treasury Alexander Hamilton was accepted as President Washington's representative, and the Federalist majority in Congress was maintained by meetings (caucuses) of Hamilton and other members of "the government" with those members of Congress labeled as government supporters or Federalists—as distinguished from others who thought of themselves as Republicans (more frequently and derisively called Democrats). Symbolic of this parliamentary arrangement was the practice of Presidents Washington and Adams, who delivered the State of the Union message personally to Congress in joint session. After 1801 President Jefferson terminated this practice, and presidents until Woodrow Wilson sent the State of the Union message to Congress, where it was read by a clerk.

This parliamentary form of politics extended to control of the presidential selection process. Although the Constitution provided explicitly for presidential election only and was silent on selection (that is, nomination), a brief review of the three basic features of presidential selection during the regime

11

of the founding will demonstrate that the so-called electoral college was designed as the nominating process, and the House of Representatives was designed to be the actual election mechanism. The pattern is so pronounced that it could hardly have happened without intention.

The original process of selection began with state legislatures selecting electors according to Article II, section 1, by whatever manner they chose. In the first election for Washington in 1788, for example, electors were chosen by the legislature in seven states and by voters in six states. Also according to constitutional prescription, the electors, once chosen, were to meet in their state capitals and *only* in their state capitals. There is no such thing as an "electoral college"; that term is to be found neither in the Constitution nor in the *Federalist Papers*. Hamilton in *Federalist* No. 68 cites as one of the virtues of the process that electors are a state institution without any national gathering whatsoever.

The second feature, also prescribed by Article II, was the right and obligation of each elector to cast ballots for *two persons*—not two votes but separate votes for two persons, one of whom was not to be from the same state as the elector. The candidate with the most electoral votes would be declared president if the number of votes exceeded an absolute majority (that is, a majority of all the electoral votes). The candidate with the second largest electoral vote would be declared vice president.

The third feature has to do with what happened when there was no absolute majority for a candidate. In that event, the *top five names* would be sent to the House of Representatives, where each state would have a single vote, regardless of its population.

The intention of this arrangement seems to be quite clear. Without a national meeting and with each elector having to cast ballots for two persons, it was to be expected that more than five names for president would ordinarily emerge. (The concept of the "favorite son" actually goes back to George Washington himself and came to be understood as a reference to a presidential candidate well known and strongly favored in one or more states of a particular section of the United States.) Surely all of this means that the House of Representatives would ordinarily make the final choice for president.

What the Constitution actually provided was a two-tiered presidential selection system, with *nomination* by the electors and *election* by the House of Representatives. This has all the makings of a parliamentary system, regardless of whether parties were going to form and regardless of whether there were to be two parties or three or more. It has parliamentarism written all over it, and there is nothing inconsistent between this and the principle of separation of powers, unless that principle is defined as some kind of system of three totally separated branches without a common trunk. For the building of a new nation-state, leadership was in the executive; yet all the powers were lodged in Congress. What better resolution than a modified parliamentarism with a strong executive elected by the lower house?

The Regime of Patronage

Jefferson was for the most part a strong president in direct line with his two predecessors, and to a large extent he exercised his power in a parliamentary way. His secretary of the Treasury, Albert Gallatin, for example, looked a great deal like Alexander Hamilton as the administrative leader of the party's caucus in the House. Jefferson named his own floor leader, who was also chairman of the all-important Committee on Ways and Means. But all this was coming unstuck well before Jefferson left office. Jefferson's administration proved to be a period of transition between the regime of the founding and the regime of patronage.

Beginning in the early 1800s, the typical congressional output shifted fundamentally away from one-time-only, state-building policies to large numbers of highly particularized routine and repeatable congressional enactments. Table 2 maps these out in relation to the more important functions being performed by the state governments.

The feature common to all the national policies of that period is *patronage* if we understand that term in its proper sense of "to patronize" rather than according to its popular definition as the mere passing out of jobs to the faithful. To patronize is to distribute resources on a highly particularized, individual basis, with each unit of patronage given as a reward for past favors, as a price of loyalty for future purposes, or simply as a response to a request thought to be meritorious. This so well describes the prevalent form of activity of the national government all during the nineteenth century that the regime itself can be appropriately entitled the regime of patronage.

By whatever title, this kind of regime was intended by the framers for the national government. These are the powers "expressly delegated" to the national government by Article I, section 8.

Governmentally, the regime of patronage was Congress centered. The beginning of the end for strong presidents and parliamentarism was the emergence of the standing committee system, and the engine of congressional supremacy was the party system. Although there was some continuity of membership in the parties throughout the period, these parties of the regime of patronage were distinctive. Whereas the original parties were strongly programmatic, even ideological, the parties of the regime of patronage were nothing more or less than patronage parties. This fact has been noted by any number of scholars; European scholars have always been shocked to learn that the American party system of the nineteenth century could be so effective without any ideological or programmatic bases at all.[2] Very quickly national

TABLE 2

FUNCTIONS OF THE NATIONAL GOVERNMENT AND OF THE STATES IN THE
TRADITIONAL SYSTEM, 1804–1939

National Government Policies (Domestic)	State Government Functions
Internal improvements	Property laws (including slavery)
Subsidies	Estate and inheritance laws
Tariffs	Commerce laws (ownership and exchange)
Public lands disposal	Banking and credit laws
Patents	Insurance laws
Coinage	Family laws
	Morals laws
	Public health and quarantine laws
	Education laws
	General penal laws
	Public works laws (including eminent domain)
	Construction codes
	Land-use laws
	Water and mineral resources laws
	Judiciary and criminal procedure laws
	Electoral laws (including political parties)
	Local government laws
	Civil service laws
	Occupations and professions laws

politics had shifted from parliamentary or institutional democracy to party democracy.

The most dramatic manifestation of this transition to party democracy was the displacement of the so-called electoral college. This displacement had begun with the "crisis of 1800," when, by an unexpected display of party discipline, the electors produced a tie vote between Republican candidates Thomas Jefferson and Aaron Burr. The Twelfth Amendment put an end to that kind of crisis by providing separate ballots for president and vice president and by reducing the runoff from the top five to the top three presidential candidates when no candidate won an absolute majority of the electors. The framers of the Twelfth Amendment apparently hoped to salvage the electoral college by discouraging all but a few candidates. Allowing five candidates in the runoff encourages a large number of candidates because each can see a good chance of getting the 20 percent (or less) of the vote necessary to squeak into the runoff in the House. Reducing the runoff to the top three candidates significantly raised the threshold conditions, thereby

14

giving party leaders an opportunity to discourage candidates whose support was limited to no more than one or two states.

Like the political reforms of the 1960s and 1970s, however, the Twelfth Amendment actually facilitated the very thing it sought to prevent—disciplined, majoritarian, opportunistic patronage parties. For about twenty years the nomination of candidates for president came into the sole possession of the party members in Congress, meeting as a conference or caucus. This came to be called King Caucus, but it was the transitional nominating system, lasting only about twenty years. The presidential nominating convention displaced the more elitist King Caucus as soon as the parties had voters in a significant number of districts where they did not elect a member of Congress. After 1832 there was no longer any need to send the top three candidates to the House of Representatives for election.

The convention system of nomination lasted for at least 120 years because the system of patronage parties lasted about that long, and patronage parties endured as long as the *regime* of patronage endured. The transition through King Caucus lasted a good twenty years, but eventually the patronage system of government and the patronage system of politics came into consonance with each other, reinforcing each other for over a century.

The Regime of Regulation and Redistribution

The third regime emerged out of the New Deal, not from the increased size of the national government but from the addition of new functions, new at least to the national government. As can be seen in table 3, the traditional patronage functions continued, but significant advances occurred with and after the New Deal. Although occasional regulatory and redistributive policies had been enacted between the late 1880s and 1914, these were few and far between until the New Deal. The Supreme Court dispelled almost all remaining constitutional doubt by the late 1930s.

With the adoption of regulatory and redistributive policies on a large scale, the national government fundamentally revised its relationship to American citizens. Until this point in American history, the direct, coercive functions of government were performed by the states—exercising what jurists call the police power. With the New Deal the national government also became directly and coercively involved with citizens. The states continued governing as they had to govern traditionally; there was no question of usurpation. The national government did not take anything from the states but added regulatory and redistributive functions of its own.

Congress did more than enact the new policies that gave the national government its new function and its·new relation to citizens. What made the new regime particularly distinctive was the manner in which Congress enacted those policies. Congress did not attempt to provide a clear rule of law in each

TABLE 3

THE POLITICAL ECONOMY OF THE NEW DEAL: HIGHLIGHTS OF POLICY
ACTIVITY, 1939–

Patronage policies
    Civil Works Administration (CWA) 1933
    Civilian Conservation Corps (CCC) 1933
    Public Works Administration (PWA) 1933
    Rural Electrification Administration (REA) 1933
    Tennessee Valley Authority (TVA) 1933
    Works Progress Administration (WPA) 1933
    Soil Conservation Service (SCS) 1935

Regulatory policies
    Agricultural Adjustment Act (AAA) 1933
    Banking Act 1933
    National Industrial Recovery Act 1933
    Securities Act 1934
    Securities Exchange Act 1934
    National Labor Relations Act 1935
    Public Utilities Holding Company Act 1935
    Bituminous Coal Act 1935 and 1937
    Federal Power Act 1935
    Civil Aeronautics Act 1938
    Fair Labor Standards Act (FLSA) 1938
    Federal Trade Commission (FTC) expansion 1938
    Food and Drug Act (FDA) expansion 1938

Redistributive policies
    Bank holiday 1933
    Federal Deposit Insurance Corporation (FDIC) 1933
    Home Owners Loan Corporation (HOLC) 1933
    Devaluation Act 1934
    Federal Housing Administration (FHA) 1934
    Farm Security Administration (FSA) 1935
    Federal Reserve reforms 1935
    Internal Revenue reforms 1935
    Social Security act 1935
    Public Housing 1939

of the new policies but instead broadly identified the contours of the problem and delegated to the executive branch virtually all the discretion necessary to formulate the actual rules to be imposed on citizens to implement each of the new policies. Technically, this procedure is called the delegation of power, and the rationalization was that Congress had indeed passed the law and the administrative agencies were expected only to fill in the details. But almost everyone knew that the executive branch was filling in more than details. In effect, whether by intention or not, the delegation of power from Congress to the executive branch created a new system of government for the new policies of regulation and redistribution. Just as Woodrow Wilson could appropriately epitomize the national government of the nineteenth century as *congressional government* (and could write a book with that title), we can with no greater distortion entitle the regime following the New Deal *presidential government.*

The first efforts to adapt national politics to the changed regime were abortive, because President Franklin D. Roosevelt attempted to build the popular base for presidential government on a virtually revolutionized party, a true programmatic party. It began with the change in 1936 of the century-old two-thirds rule for nominating presidential candidates to the Democratic party, a reform aimed at wiping out the power of a minority of the party to dictate the presidential nomination or the terms of that nomination. The issue of reconstituting the party came to a head in the famous "purge of 1938," in which Roosevelt rejected all the traditional norms of party politics and declared war on the conservative leaders of his own party by opposing their renomination during the spring and summer before the 1938 Senate and House elections. History records that Roosevelt failed and his effort backfired. But the actual lessons Roosevelt learned were that (1) *the president cannot depend on locally organized patronage parties and* (2) *the modern presidency needs its own, independent base of popular support.*

Having encountered entirely too much resistance in his effort to build a true programmatic party, Roosevelt turned away from the patronage parties almost altogether toward another kind of effort that was already beginning to pay off: building a popular base directly among the voters, through the media of mass communication. History records that he became a master performer on the radio and a master manipulator of the national newspapers and news services. That is probably true, but there is more to the story than that: the new functions of the national government and the personal responsibility of the president to carry out those new functions and, through them, to set the whole world to rights brought the attention of the entire American public into focus on the presidency and the president. The president's constituency became the public en masse, and that in turn shaped the politics of the new regime.

Although the signs of the decay of party democracy were, therefore, fairly prominent earlier, 1952 is probably the best single year in which to locate the irreversible turning point. Facts about 1952 are commonplace; for that very reason, their importance as a connection between the post–New Deal form of government and the post–New Deal form of politics is not so well appreciated.

The presidential conventions of 1952 were the last classic conventions, where parties still controlled the nominations through the control of state party leaders over the delegates in their delegations. As a former Tammany leader described the traditional pattern: "The first thing a candidate who wants a nomination from a convention should realize is that the delegates themselves are not free agents, nor are they individuals subject to persuasion. . . . In short, the delegate is the property of his leader."[3]

As the 1952 Republican National Convention approached, the forces of Dwight Eisenhower had to confront the fact that Robert Taft was ahead in firm delegate commitments. Bold moves were called for, and the move they chose proved to be revolutionary. They officially questioned the credentials of several state delegations whose members, pledged to Taft, had been selected by the traditional method of virtual appointment by the state party leaders. When the Eisenhower leaders went before the credentials committee of the Republican National Convention and failed to move that committee (whose officials were all carefully selected by Taft), they took their objections to the convention floor in the form of a "fair play" motion. This motion not only opposed the seating of certain Taft delegations; it went further by proposing that delegates whose credentials were in question not be permitted to vote on any motion until their own right to sit had been settled.

The debate took place over national television—despite Taft's objections—and the Eisenhower motion swayed enough neutral delegations to gain the majority vote on the contested delegations and to impress enough delegates ultimately to win the presidential nomination. But more important than the immediate gain for Eisenhower was the long-range result, which was to weaken further the foundations of the traditional party system itself. From that time onward, delegates came to be treated as factors in their own right, as individuals to be courted rather than as pawns in a state delegation controlled by state party leaders. Once the delegates became meaningful individuals, the process of selection had to be democratized.

This is where the primaries came in. The practice of electing delegates pledged in advance to a particular presidential candidate contributed to the decline of traditional parties. But the traditional practice in which the delegate was the "property of his leader" *was already seriously undermined before the significant spread of selection of pledged delegates by primary elections.* To that extent the primaries are as much a reflection as a cause of the decline of party control of the presidential selection process. And, although the rise and spread of primaries with pledged delegates is the most palpable development of the past thirty years, that should not mask the more fundamental fact, which is that the entire structure of party has come unstuck. Presidential nomination has become an open process by which candidates *amass* individual delegates, who have very little in common with one another or with the candidate to whom they are pledged. The result of this process is not a coalition at all but a "flux" of individual delegates who revolve around the candidate and have nothing else in common.

Serious students of American political parties have been arguing for more than a decade over whether the political reforms of the 1960s and 1970s were a cause of party decline or a reflection of the decline already well on the road. I tend to accept the latter argument, but what matters is that we are experiencing the slow but sure emergence of a new form of politics consonant with the regime of regulation and redistribution and with presidential government. Just as it took twenty to twenty-five years for party democracy to emerge and institutionalize itself in congressional dominance and the convention system of selecting presidents, so it is taking twenty or more years for its replacement to emerge.

Since we are still in the midst of the transformation, the ultimate form is anybody's guess. Reasonable estimates as well as appropriate reforms to hasten it or to head it off will not take place, however, unless we recognize the significance of the transformation and the causes of it that lie deep within the regime itself. To contribute to a livelier discourse, I will give my own view of this transformation in a somewhat exaggerated version, which is that *party democracy is dead*. Although conditions vary from one state to another, those variations have little bearing on national politics. In fact, part of the current transformation is the virtual severance of national from state and local politics toward a federalism of politics in which the two layers are more separate from each other than the two layers of government were when constitutional federalism was more strict.

Once again, 1952 was something of a turning point, marked by Eisenhower's initiating, permitting, or encouraging the formation of the Citizens for Eisenhower. Within twenty years, with the formation of CRP (Committee to Re-Elect the President) for Richard Nixon, presidential candidates and presidents consistently followed the Eisenhower precedent by forming their own personal organizations, using them in the competition for delegates, and then using the same organizations to conduct the campaign for president, independent of the campaigns and candidates for all the other offices in all the other elections. Kennedy confirmed the practice a decade before Nixon by going outside the regular party leadership, enlisting political amateurs, and forcing himself on what remained of the party to have a following he could claim as his own—all this despite the fact that Kennedy was a product of party politics.

It was really the Republicans, however, who institutionalized the separate and independent political organization for president, and that is most of the explanation for the tremendous success of Republicans in the presidency coupled with their lack of equivalent progress in state and local affairs. Republicans have won four of the past five presidential elections, two of them by majorities of historic magnitude, without significantly piercing the outer crust of national politics into state, local, and congressional domains.

This is no accident but a direct result of the efforts of the past five presidents to create a mass political base for themselves and their administration. President Ronald Reagan's 1984 strategy was consistent, despite the virtual certainty of his victory and despite the bitter complaints against this strategy by state and local candidates. Here is how stalwart Republican Robert Michel, House minority leader, put the case against Reagan hours after the 1984 election: "He never really, in my opinion, joined that issue of what it really means to have the numbers in the House. . . . Here the son-of-a-buck ended up with 59% and you bring in [only 14]seats."[4]

In the emerging mass democracy, party leaders are replaced by public relations and communications experts. Professional politicians and party strategists are replaced by pollsters. Campaigning is replaced by marketing. Local canvassing continues but is transformed from competition for personal contact to competition for demographic and attitudinal information to plug into the candidate's (or president's) national data bank. The requirement of fifty separate state nominating processes is under siege, and the post-1984 reform movement could succeed in replacing it with regional primaries or four "super Tuesdays," in which all states within a region or time zone would be required to hold their state selections, or with a single national primary, or with a designating convention followed by a national runoff primary. But whatever happens, even if it be maintenance of the present system, national politics will have been transformed into some variant of mass democracy, because mass democracy has proved to be consonant with the regime of regulation and redistribution and with presidential government.

None of this means that national parties are literally, physically disappearing. That is not the way of human institutions. The national parties continue to do essentially what they did for over a century. But what they do is no longer sufficient to control presidential selection and to play a major role in the national administration. Ironically, the party base for presidential power was weakening toward collapse just as presidents began to need it.

Some observers are now arguing that the two parties are making a comeback, and they cite the remarkable success of the Republican National Committee (RNC) in organizing for data collection, fund raising, and distribution of resources to significant marginal districts. And Democrats are paying Republicans the supreme compliment: imitation. If the RNC succeeds and the Democratic National Committee (DNC) follows suit, however, the parties they make will be a far cry from the ones they left behind two or three decades ago. First, there is no sign that the headquarters of the parties have recaptured or can recapture the presidency through the reassertion of influence in the presidential nominating process. Without that they can neither be near presidential power nor serve effectively as the popular base for presidential power. Second, even if they should regain so much as a foothold in the presidential sphere, parties in the current RNC mold would still be built from the top down, dealing in masses of data, masses of names and addresses, through computerized retrieval and analysis, mass mailings, and expenditures mainly to meet the gigantic financial burden of mass communication. This describes neither a traditional American patronage party nor a European programmatic or ideological party, although the Republican party now comes closer to the latter than to the former.

If we project the RNC and DNC strategy toward a successful conclusion, we can envisage a replacement of our patronage parties with "taxation parties"—parties whose primary function will be identifying and attracting the people who will serve as sponsors. Even without the federal finance laws that provide sanctions and incentives for seeking out a large number of small contributors, the new taxation parties, especially the Republican party, would probably have organized to reach the smaller contributors, not because they wish to avoid being labeled the party of the rich but because this action serves the dual purpose of fund raising and vote solicitation.

We could also call these taxation parties "progressive-type" parties because they resemble in their purpose and their social composition the political parties sought by reformers called progressives in the early part of this century—that is, parties that progressives sought but did not quite get because they sought parties that would destroy themselves. The goal was to use such democratizing reforms as direct primaries, voter registration, government-run elections, the short ballot, and the merit system to take politics away from the working classes on behalf of the middle classes, moving politics from parties of people and petty patronage (including obscure jobs with low skill demands) to a nonparty politics of personality and symbols administered by government agencies. As Ginsberg and Shefter, among others, find the middle classes and special organizations of middle-class interests back of the progressive reforms, so do Nelson Polsby and others confirm similar outcomes and probably similar motives today.[5]

The "mass parties" of Europe arose out of the working class; they were socialist and social democratic parties, whose success in organizing voters around ideology and programs produced similar organizations on the right. This process was called "contagion from the left." The "mass parties" of the United States of the 1980s and beyond are, if the present efforts succeed, a "contagion from the right," and the principles of organization will probably hold up only as long as the Republican leadership remains ideologically right wing. If, however, Republican leadership returns to the nonideological, pragmatic, mainstream Republicanism, the mass party being constructed by those who now dominate will not hold together. If it holds together, it will be a moral minority party in what is likely to become a national three- or four-party system. If, as is more likely, it does not hold together, the two-party system will persist as a vestigial organ composed of two clusters of partisan attitudes shifting at the margins in response to the personalities and strategies of presidential candidates and their personal organizations.

The reforms of the 1960s and 1970s, begun in the Democratic party but quickly and in largest part copied by the Republicans, were basically antiparty reforms, and they accelerated the trend away from party democracy just as the Twelfth Amendment unintentionally accelerated the trend toward party democracy. But in neither instance can one say that the reforms caused the trend. The direct cause in both cases was the transformation of the regime—the transformation of the Constitution and the functions of government. Thus, if I am even partially correct in tying mass democracy to the regulatory and redistributive regime and to presidential government, then the prospects for restoring and strengthening party democracy are very poor. The prospects are even drearier if the effort to restore party democracy continues to concentrate on reforms of party selection processes or campaign financing. We have seen in all too many studies the counterproductive and unwanted consequences of well-intentioned party and campaign reforms.

Nothing perverse is at work here: the reforms do not work or are actually counterproductive because *the influence of the plebiscitary presidency in the new regime is far stronger than any reforms working merely through parties.* No progress away from mass democracy toward renewed party democracy can be made through the province of the parties themselves. No substantial and lasting construction of the desperately needed party democracy can take place without a direct confrontation with the regime itself, especially presidential government.

This means constitutional change. Political change will follow. To reverse that process is grabbing the tail to wag the dog. The founders believed that a good Constitution is its own political solution. They had a superior grasp of the principle that regimes govern politics. Moreover, they recognized something else we often forget: that constitutional change is vital to constitutional stability and, further, that each generation inherits the right of constitution making and state building.

A total rewriting of the Constitution in a new constitutional convention is unnecessary. Given the poverty of American experience with constitutional change in our generation, a constitutional convention is downright perilous, because too few people will understand and respect the limits of a constitution and many will try to embed all sorts of legislation in it. The last major constitutional changes were triggered by the New Deal and were made without a single constitutional amendment.

The lesson applies today and with promise of superior results if we are more conscious than the New Dealers of what we are doing and why. To confront presidential government with its mass politics and its jealousy of party democracy is to alter—I would say to raise—the discourse toward the real problem. How much longer will reformers continue to try to restore parties through party reform before they discover that the tail they are chasing is their own?

Notes

1. Joseph Charles, *The Origins of the American Party System* (New York: Harper and Row, Torchbooks, 1961); and Noble E. Cunningham, *The Jeffersonian Republicans: The Formation of Party Organization, 1789–1801* (Chapel Hill: University of North Carolina Press, 1957).

2. A lively and approving treatment of the patronage parties will be found in Herbert Agar, *The Price of Union* (Boston: Houghton Mifflin, 1966).

3. Edward N. Costikyan, *Behind Closed Doors: Politics in the Public Interest* (New York: Harcourt, Brace & World, 1966), pp. 166–67.

4. Quoted in Richard Viguerie, "Reagan's Campaign Double-crossed the GOP," *New York Times*, November 12, 1984.

5. Benjamin Ginsberg, *The Consequences of Consent* (Boston: Addison-Wesley, 1982), p. 146; Martin Shefter, "Party Bureaucracy and Political Change," in Louis Maisel and Joseph Cooper, eds., *Political Parties: Development and Decay* (Beverly Hills, Calif.: Sage Publications, 1978), chap. 7; and Nelson Polsby, *Consequences of Party Reform* (New York: Oxford University Press, 1983).

The Case for the Current Presidential Nominating Process

Michael Nelson

The current process by which Americans nominate their parties' candidates for president is the product of nearly two centuries of historical evolution and two decades of deliberate procedural reform. It can be judged successful because it satisfies reasonably well the three main criteria by which any presidential nominating process may be judged:

• Does the process strengthen or weaken the two major parties, which our political system relies on to provide some measure of coherence to a constitutionally fragmented government?

• Does the process foster or impede the selection of presidents who are suitably skilled for the office?

• Is the process regarded as legitimate by the public? Is it seen to be fair and democratic?

Political Parties

Have the two major parties been weakened by the reforms of the presidential nominating process that were instituted by the McGovern-Fraser commission and its successors? Much scholarly talent and energy have been devoted to answering this question in the affirmative. Implicit in such analyses are the beliefs that the parties were basically strong before the post-1968 reforms and that they have been considerably weaker ever since. In truth, neither of these beliefs is fully accurate. The parties were in a state of decline during the 1950s and 1960s, a decline that has been arrested and in most cases reversed during the 1970s and 1980s, as the parties, aided by the reforms, have adapted to the changed social and political environment that underlay their decline. This is true of all three of the components of parties that political scientists, following V.O. Key, have identified as fundamental: the party-in-the-electorate, the party-in-government, and the party organization.[1]

Party-in-the-Electorate. Americans are no longer as loyal to the parties as they were in the early 1950s, when modern survey research on voting behavior first took form. On this there is little room for dispute: as figure 1 indicates, voters are far less likely now than in the past to think of themselves as either Democrats or Republicans, to vote a straight-party ticket (even for presidential and House candidates), or to express a favorable evaluation of one or both political parties.

FIGURE 1

INDEXES OF PARTY STRENGTH, 1952–1984

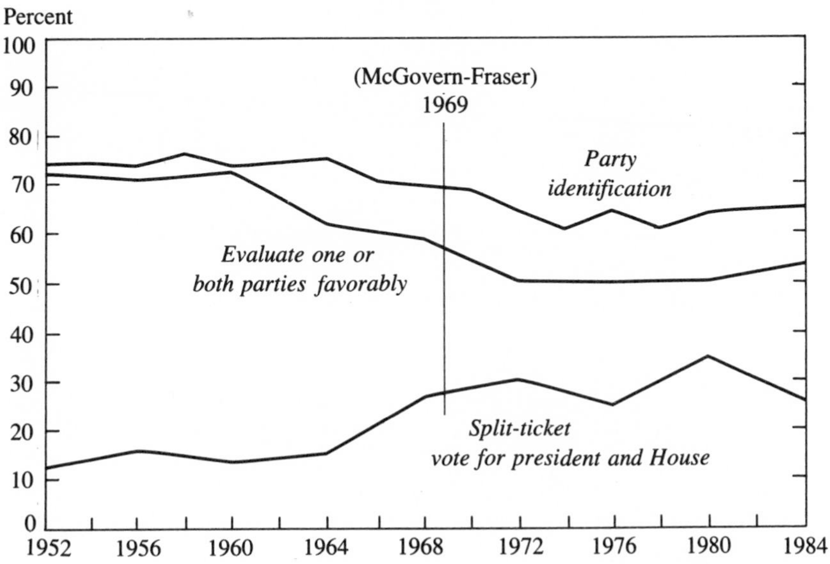

SOURCES: Stephen J. Wayne, *The Road to the White House*, 2d ed. (New York: St. Martin's Press, 1984), pp. 57, 59; David E. Price, *Bringing Back the Parties* (Washington, D.C.: Congressional Quarterly Press, 1984), p. 18; and Martin P. Wattenberg, "Realignment without Party Revitalization" (unpublished manuscript).

Natural though the tendency may be to explain dramatic changes by equally dramatic causes, one cannot attribute the decline of the party-in-the-electorate to the reform era that began in 1968. The largest falloff in party identification, which had remained steadily high through the 1950s and early 1960s, came between 1964 and 1966. An additional large drop occurred between 1970 and 1972, but since then the decline in party identification seems to have leveled off or even been reversed. The share of voters who evaluate at least one party favorably, which fell steadily during the 1960s, has stayed very close to 50 percent ever since, rising to 52 percent in 1984. Similarly, split-ticket voting, a more explicitly behavioral indicator of weak voter loyalty to the parties, underwent its greatest increases before the reform era and has declined since 1980.

Whether Ronald Reagan's presidency has reversed the "dealignment" of voters that occurred mainly during the 1960s remains to be seen. But well before 1980 most of the indexes of party strength in the electorate at least had stopped falling.

Party-in-Government. Historically, Americans have used the political parties to join what the Constitution put asunder, namely, the executive and legislative branches. The electorate's habit of straight-ticket voting in twentieth-century elections before 1956 meant that the party that controlled the White House also controlled both houses of Congress in forty-six of fifty-four years.

The rise of split-ticket voting weakened such interbranch aspects of party-in-government: nowadays control by the same party of the presidency and Congress is the exception rather than the rule. As with the party-in-the-electorate, however, the evidence indicates that the party-weakening trend in government began well before the reform era: indeed, it was in 1954 that the new pattern of Republican presidents and divided or Democratic congresses emerged.

Even more significant than the trend in interbranch party strength, perhaps, is the intrabranch trend. During the supposedly halcyon days of parties in the 1950s and 1960s, party unity voting in Congress, as measured by the *Congressional Quarterly*, declined fairly steadily in both parties in both houses, bottoming out in the Ninety-first Congress. During the 1970s and 1980s, in direct contradiction to what the "reform-killed-the-parties" theory would predict, party unity voting has been on the increase. (So has the share of all congressional votes that unite one party against the other.) Nor has this intrabranch development been devoid of interbranch consequences: in 1981 Senate Republicans demonstrated the highest degree of support for a president ever recorded by either party in either house of Congress since the *Congressional Quarterly* began making measurements in 1953.[2]

Party Organization. It is as organizations that the parties were affected most directly by the post-1968 reforms; if party-weakening effects are to be found anywhere, it should be in the realm of party organization. Yet it is here, recent research increasingly is showing, that the opposite is most true: the parties in the 1970s and 1980s are institutionally stronger than they were in the 1950s and 1960s.

The regeneration of the parties as organizations has occurred at all levels of the federal system. In the localities and counties there is now far more party activity in the areas of fund raising, campaign headquarters, voter registration, and get-out-the-vote efforts than during the mid-1960s. About twice as many citizens as in the 1950s (some 24 to 32 percent) report that they have been approached personally by party workers in recent presidential campaigns. The share of state party organizations that have permanent headquarters rose from less than half in 1960 to 95 percent in 1982; the size and professionalism of salaried state party staffs have also grown considerably. Judging from his study of party budgets, political scientist Cornelius Cotter concludes that the percentage of state parties whose organization is "marginal" fell from 69 in 1961 to 31 in 1979; the proportion of highly organized state parties rose from 12 percent to 26 percent.

National party organizations, long the stepchild of the party system, have undergone the most striking transformation of all. Since the mid-1970s, when William Brock became chairman, the Republican National Committee has developed a capacity to recruit candidates to run for local office and provide them with funds and professional assistance in such activities as voter registration and television campaigning; to help state parties enhance their own organizational abilities; to do institutional advertising on a "Vote Republican" theme; and so on. As for the opposition, journalist David Broder reports, "Since 1980 the Democrats have been doing what the Republicans did under Brock: raising money and pumping it back to party-building projects at the state and local level."[3]

The Fall and Rise of the Parties. Political parties in the 1980s have arrested or reversed the decline that they were suffering before the reform era that began in 1968 but only because they are different from what they used to be. The recent reforms have helped the parties to adapt relatively successfully to a changing social and political environment.

Organizationally and procedurally, the parties on the eve of the post-1968 reforms were relics of an earlier era. Virtually since the Andrew Jackson years, party strength had continued to rest on the same foundations. Patronage, in the form of government jobs and contracts, had long been one reliable source of workers and funds for party organizations. Party-sponsored charity work—memorably, the Thanksgiving turkey and the winter bucket of coal—helped to cement the loyalties of many voters. Such tangible inducements aside, voters also found the party label the best device for ordering their choices in elections that involved numerous offices, candidates, and issues.

For some years before 1968, developments in government and society had been weakening these foundations. A merit-based civil service and competitive contracting replaced the patronage system of government hiring and purchasing. Income security programs reduced dependence on charity. After World War II education, income, and leisure time rose rapidly throughout the population—voters now had more ability and opportunity to sort out information for themselves about candidates and issues. During the 1950s television sets became fixtures in the American home, bringing such information to voters in more accessible (if not always more valuable) form.

From these developments, which eroded some of the main props of the traditional political parties, came others that created the basis for new-style parties. First, the issue basis of political participation intensified, both in the movements of the 1960s (civil rights, antiwar, environmental, feminist, and others), which originated mainly outside the party system, and in the parties themselves. In 1962 James Q. Wilson chronicled the rise during the 1950s of the "amateur Democrat," an upper-middle-class reformer whose main concern was for issues and who saw the party as a vehicle for advancing causes, in opposition to professional party people, who viewed elections mainly as a means of achieving the satisfactions and spoils of victory. In 1964 the amateur Democrat's conservative Republican cousin, whom Aaron Wildavsky dubbed the "purist," seized control of the Republican national convention.[4]

Second, the candidate basis of politics intensified, both in presidential politics, where individual aspirants, following John F. Kennedy in 1960, sought to take their own popular paths to the nomination even if that meant detouring around the party professionals, and in congressional politics, where reelection-oriented incumbents, with increasing success, forged personal bonds with their constitutents that freed them from much of their dependency on party. Finally, the media basis of politics intensified. As television, radio, and direct mail became available and highly effective routes for reaching voters, media professionals became more valuable politically, as did fund-raising specialists who could help to pay for the expensive new forms of campaigning.

Political parties in all their aspects—in the electorate, in government, and as organizations—were weakened during the 1950s and 1960s by these social and political developments. To recover and thrive the parties had to adapt. To adapt they had to accommodate the rise of four main groups: new-style voters, who by virtue of greater education and leisure no longer needed to depend on parties to order their choices in elections; amateur political activists who regarded the parties mainly as vehicles for political change; entrepreneurial candidates who had ceased to regard party fealty as the necessary or even the most desirable strategy for electoral success; and modern political tacticians who practiced the now essential crafts of polling, advertising, press relations, and fund raising. In sum, the reinvigoration of the parties would have to come on terms that accepted the "new politics" in both that label's common uses: policy as the basis for political participation, and modern campaign professionalism as the incentive to channel such participation through the parties.

What made the transformation and reinvigoration of the parties possible was the organizational and procedural fluidity that was hastened by the post-1968 reforms. Once the lingering hold of party professionals of the *ancien régime* on the nominating process was broken, the new groups of voters, activists, candidates, and campaign professionals were able to establish a new equilibrium of power within the parties that reflected the changed social and political realities. Republicans realized this first and strengthened their party by committing it to conservative political ideology and professional campaign services, which in turn tied the party-in-the-electorate, the party-in-government, and the party organization together. Democrats, preoccupied with the reform process more than with the fruits of reform, were slower to adapt. But, responding to the Republican party's success, they now seem to be following a parallel path: new policies and a new professionalism to rebuild the party.

Perhaps the best evidence of the parties' successful adaptation to change is that the old amateurs have become the new professionals: committed to policy but also to party. Summarizing several studies of delegates to recent Republican and Democratic national conventions, William Crotty and John Jackson conclude that "the new professionals are likely to be college graduates working in a service profession . . . familiar with all the paraphernalia of modern campaigning . . . [and] likely to care deeply about at least some issues. . . . They also care, sometimes passionately, about their party . . . and they see the parties as the best vehicles for advancing both their concept of the public interest and their own political careers."[5]

Presidents

Many political analysts have argued vigorously that the influence of the presidential nominating process on the selection of suitably skilled presidents, like its influence on the parties, was benign before the post-1968 reforms were instituted but has been malignant ever since. "In the old way," according to Broder, "whoever wanted to run for president of the United States took a couple of months off from public service in the year of the presidential election and presented his credentials to the leaders of his party, who were elected officials, party officials, leaders of allied interest groups, and bosses in some cases. These people had known the candidate over a period of time and had carefully examined his work."[6] As it happened, the qualities those political peers were looking for, argues political scientist Jeane Kirkpatrick, were the very qualities that make for good presidents: "the ability to deal with diverse groups, ability to work out compromises, and the ability to impress people who have watched a candidate over many years." In contrast, under the post-1968 rules, "the skills required to be successful in the nominating process are almost entirely irrelevant to, perhaps even negatively correlated with, the skills required to be successful at governing."[7]

In a real sense, the old nominating process did work reasonably well to increase the chances of selecting skillful presidents. But then so does the new process. The difference underlying this similarity is the contrast between the political and social environment in which contemporary presidents must try to govern and the environment in which their predecessors as recently as the 1950s and 1960s had to operate.

The contrast is most obvious and significant in the nation's capital. As Samuel Kernell notes, the "old" Washington that was described so accurately by Richard Neustadt in his 1960 success manual for presidents, *Presidential Power*, was "a city filled with hierarchies. To these hierarchies were attached leaders or at least authoritative representatives"[8]—committee chairmen and party leaders in Congress, press barons, umbrella-style interest groups that represented broad sectors such as labor, business, and agriculture, and so on. In this setting to lead was to bargain—the same political "whales," to use Harry MacPherson's term, who could thwart a president's desires could also satisfy them, and in the same way: by directing the activities of their associates and followers. Clearly a presidential nominating process that placed some emphasis on a candidate's ability to pass muster with Washington power brokers was functional for the governing system.

As the 1960s drew to a close, however, the same social and political changes—and some others as well—that were undermining the foundations of the old party system also were undermining the old ways of conducting the nation's business in Washington. The capital came under the intense and—to many elected politicians—alluring spotlight of television news; a more educated and active citizenry took its heightened policy concerns directly to government officials; interest group activity both flourished and fragmented; and careerism among members of Congress prompted a steady devolution of legislative power to individual representatives and senators and to proliferating committees and subcommittees. From the president's perspective this wave of decentralization meant that Washington had become "a city of free agents" in which "the number of exchanges necessary to secure others' support ha[d] increased dramatically."[9]

What skills do contemporary presidents need if they are to lead in this changed environment, or, to phrase the question more pertinently, what skills should the presidential nominating process foster?[10] Two presidential leadership requirements are familiar and longstanding: first, a strategic sense of the public's disposition to be led during the particular term of office—an ability to sense, shape, and fulfill the historical possibilities of the time; second, some talent for the management of authority, both of lieutenants in the administration who can help the president form policy proposals and of the large organizations in the bureaucracy that are charged with implementing existing programs. Other skills required by presidents are more recent in origin, at least in the form they must take and their importance. Presidents must be able to present themselves and their policies to the public through rhetoric and symbolic action, especially on television. Because reelection-oriented members of Congress "are hypersensitive to anticipated constituent reaction," it is not surprising that the best predictor of a president's success with Congress is his standing in the public opinion polls.[11] Finally, presidents need tactical skills of bargaining, persuasion, and other forms of political gamesmanship to maximize their support among other officials whose help they need to secure their purposes. But in the new Washington these tactical skills must be employed not merely or even mainly on the sort of old-style power brokers who used to be able to help presidents sustain reliable coalitions but on the many elements of a fragmented power system in which tactics must be improvised for new coalitions on each issue.

In several nonobvious and even inadvertent ways, the current nominating process rewards, perhaps requires, most of these skills. The process is, for would-be presidents, self-starting and complex. To a greater extent than ever before, candidates must raise money, develop appealing issues, devise shrewd campaign strategies, impress national political reporters, attract competent staff, and build active organizations largely on their own. They then must dance through a minefield of staggered and varied state primaries and caucuses, deciding and reevaluating weekly or even daily where to spend their time, money, and other resources. What better test of a president's ability to manage lieutenants and lead in a tactically skillful way in the equally complex, fragmented, and uncertain environment of modern Washington or, for that matter, the modern world?

The fluidity of the current nominating process also has opened it to Washington "outsiders." This development, although much lamented by critics of the post-1968 reforms, has done nothing more than restore the traditional place of those who have served as state governors in the ranks of plausible candidates for the presidency, thus broadening the talent pool to include more than senators and vice-presidents. (From 1960 to 1972 every major party nominee for president was a senator or a vice-president who previously had been a senator.) As chief executives of their states, governors may be presumed to have certain skills in the management of large public bureaucracies that senators do not.

Self-presentational skills also are vital for candidates in the current nominating process—not just "looking good on television" but being able to persuade skeptical journalists and others to accept one's interpretation of the complex reality of the campaign. If it does nothing else, the endless contest, which carries candidates from place to place for months and months in settings that range from living rooms to stadiums, probably sensitizes candidates to citizens in ways that uniquely facilitate the choice of a president who has a strong strategic sense of his time.

No earthly good is unalloyed, of course. The length and complexity of the current nominating process, to which so much good can be ascribed, are nonetheless sources of real distraction to incumbent presidents who face renomination challenges and to other contenders who hold public office. To be sure, the post-1968 rules cannot be blamed for all of this. Unpopular presidents have always had to battle, to some extent, for renomination; popular presidents still do not. (In 1984 Reagan not only was unopposed for his party's nomination—the first such president since 1956—but received millions of dollars in federal matching funds for his renomination "campaign.") Most challengers seem to be able to arrange time to campaign, either while holding office (Gary Hart, Alan Cranston, Ernest Hollings, and others in 1984) or by abandoning office for the sake of pursuing the presidency (Walter Mondale in 1984, Howard Baker in 1988). Still, by any standard, the same nominating process that tests a would-be president's leadership skills so well must be said to carry at least a moderate price tag.

Public

Ironically, democratic legitimacy, the paramount value sought by the post-1968 reformers, must be judged as the least achieved of the three main criteria for judging the presidential nominating process: strengthened political parties, skilled presidents, and a satisfied public. Everyone, including journalists, decries the responsibility that the hybrid nature of the process places on the media to interpret who is winning and even which candidates will be taken seriously. Few think it proper that voters in the late primary states have their choices circumscribed by the decisions of voters in Iowa, New Hampshire, and other states with early contests.

The characteristic of the current nominating process that is most corrosive of legitimacy is its sheer complexity. As Henry Mayo notes in his *Introduction to Democratic Theory*:

> If the purpose of the election is to be carried out—to enable the voter to share in political power—the voter's job must not be made more difficult and confusing for him. It ought, on the contrary, to be made as simple as the electoral machinery can be devised to make it.[12]

Yet nothing could be less descriptive of the way we choose presidential candidates. "No school, no textbook, no course of instruction," writes Theodore H. White, "could tell young Americans how their system worked." Or, as Richard Stearns, chief delegate hunter for Senator George McGovern in 1972 and Senator Edward Kennedy in 1980, put it: "I am fully confident that there aren't more than 100 people in the country who fully understand the rules."[13]

What would the public prefer? Nothing that will prove consoling to those who dislike the current process for its excesses of democracy and absence of "peer review." Overwhelmingly, citizens want to select the parties' nominees for president through national primaries: in the most recent Gallup survey on this issue, which was completed in June 1984, 67 percent were in favor, 21 percent were opposed, and 12 percent were undecided. And there are ample reasons to believe that citizens mean what they are saying. For one, the national primary idea has received consistently high support by margins ranging from two-to-one to six-to-one—in Gallup surveys that date back to 1952. More important, the direct primary is the method by which voters are accustomed to nominating almost all party candidates for almost all other offices in the federal system.

A vigorous case can be made for a national primary, and not solely because of the heightened legitimacy it would bring to the nomination process.[14] Still, there are good reasons to stay with the current arrangement. First, the very constancy of rules rewriting is in itself subversive of legitimacy. Second, it also is distracting to the parties, diverting them from the more important task of deciding what they have to offer voters. Finally, to bring the argument of this essay full circle, to the extent that the current process helps the political parties to grow stronger and the presidency to work more effectively, voters ultimately will grow not just used to it but pleased with it, and the legitimacy problem will take care of itself.

Notes

1. V.O. Key, Jr., *Politics, Parties, and Pressure Groups*, 5th ed. (New York: Thomas Y. Crowell Co., 1964).

2. Bill Keller, "Voting Record of '81 Shows the Romance and Fidelity of Reagan Honeymoon on Hill," *Congressional Quarterly Weekly Report*, January 2, 1982, p. 19. Complete *Congressional Quarterly* data on party unity voting in Congress can be found in David E. Price, *Bringing Back the Parties* (Washington, D.C.: CQ Press, 1984), p. 57.

3. The studies of party organization referred to in this paragraph are described by Price in *Bringing Back the Parties*, chap. 2.

4. James Q. Wilson, *The Amateur Democrat* (Chicago: University of Chicago Press, 1962); and Aaron Wildavsky, "The Goldwater Phenomenon," *Review of Politics* (July 1965), pp. 387–413.

5. William Crotty and John S. Jackson III, *Presidential Primaries and Nominations* (Washington, D.C.: CQ Press, 1985), pp. 122–23.

6. John Charles Daly, mod., *Choosing Presidential Candidates* (Washington, D.C.: American Enterprise Institute, 1980), pp. 2–3.

7. A. M. Mayer, "Is This Any Way to Pick a President?" *Newsweek* (October 15, 1979), p. 69; and Jeane J. Kirkpatrick et al., *The Presidential Nominating Process* (Washington, D.C.: American Enterprise Institute, 1980), p. 11.

8. Samuel Kernell, "The Presidency and the People," in Michael Nelson, ed., *The Presidency and the Political System* (Washington, D.C.: CQ Press, 1984), p. 235. Neustadt's book was published in New York by John Wiley.

9. Ibid.; and Michael Nelson, "The *Washington Community* Revisited," *Virginia Quarterly Review* (Spring 1985), pp. 189–210.

10. For a fuller discussion of presidential leadership skill, see Erwin C. Hargrove and Michael Nelson, *Presidents, Politics, and Policy* (Baltimore: Johns Hopkins University Press, 1984), chap. 4.

11. Richard Fenno, "U.S. House Members in Their Constituencies," *American Political Science Review* (September 1977), pp. 886–87; and George C. Edwards III, *Presidential Influence in Congress* (San Francisco: W. H. Freeman, 1980).

12. Henry Mayo, *Introduction to Democratic Theory* (New York: Oxford University Press, 1960), p. 73.

13. Theodore H. White, *America in Search of Itself* (New York: Harper and Row, 1982), p. 289; "Is There a Better Method of Picking Presidential Candidates?" *New York Times*, December 2, 1979.

14. Michael Nelson, "The Presidential Nominating System," in Richard J. Zeckhauser and Derek Leebaert, eds., *What Role for Government?* (Durham, N.C.: Duke University Press, 1983), pp. 34–51.

Should the Presidential Nominating System Be Changed (Again)?

Thomas E. Mann

The current system of presidential selection has few defenders. Even those who have the most reason to stand up for the nominating system as it developed in the post-1968 reform era—Democratic party and issue activists who pressed for broad-based participation and Republicans inclined to judge a set of rules by the fruits they bear (three landslide victories in the past four presidential elections)—have difficulty overlooking shortcomings in the present arrangements for nominating presidential candidates. But sharp conflicts over the values to be maximized and disagreements over probable consequences of alternative schemes have prevented any serious consideration of wholesale change. Instead, every four years the Democrats, weighing the lessons of the previous campaign and giving rein to the short-term political calculations of the new crop of presidential contenders, revise the rules of the game, while Republicans brace themselves for possible spillover effects on their nomination system.

If the presidential nominating system is to be changed in a fundamental way, proponents will have to convince competing politicians that the maladies of the present arrangements can be eliminated or substantially reduced without compromising the basic interests of those politicians or unleashing a new set of problems that make matters worse than they are now. The purpose of this essay is to review problems with the current system, constraints on major reform efforts, and the benefits and costs of alternative arrangements.

Problems with the Present System

The case for the current system of presidential nomination rests upon the same factors that are the target of the most telling criticism. The system is said to be open, deliberative, and responsive to popular preferences.[1] It is open to "one man and the truth," a candidate without extensive resources or national recognition who taps a vein of public sentiment, and open to individuals whose

35

strong feelings about a candidate or issue propel them to active participation in party affairs. It is deliberative in the sense that it is sequential, providing sufficient time and varying conditions under which candidates can be scrutinized by the media, by activists, and by the voters. It is responsive to popular preferences because presidential primaries dominate—candidates cannot win the nomination without demonstrating their appeal among the party's rank and file.

Critics see these strengths as weaknesses.[2] A system open to outsider candidates discourages responsible officeholders from seeking the nomination by putting a premium on full-time personal campaigning many months, even years, before the formal start of the state caucuses and primaries. These demands on a candidate's time and attention effectively limit the pool of political talent from which presidents are selected. A system open to issue and candidate enthusiasts denigrates the role of party regulars and public officials, reducing the influence of those concerned with long-term party fortunes, diminishing peer review of presidential candidates, and weakening the ties between campaigning and governing.

The sequential nature of the nomination process is seen by critics as producing the very opposite of a deliberative choice. The first several states receive the lion's share of candidate and media attention, and unexpected showings in Iowa and New Hampshire, even modest pluralities or second-place finishes, can generate a tide of favorable publicity that directly affects subsequent contests. As more states have moved their primaries or caucuses earlier in the season, a front-loaded system has evolved, with little breathing space in which to scrutinize candidates. It is now possible for a candidate to wrap up the nomination without the vast majority of the party's voters having any clear sense of who he is and what he stands for. The problem is compounded by the premature narrowing of the field of candidates. Only caucus participants in Iowa and primary voters in New Hampshire have a full roster of candidates from which to choose. A poor showing—one that does not meet "expectations"—in one of the early events leads to media inattention and a drying up of campaign contributions, forcing most candidates to the sidelines soon after the formal nomination season has begun. Finally, the national party conventions as now conceived deny any opportunity to deliberate among candidates. Modern conventions ratify choices made in primaries and caucuses, and delegates are merely agents for candidates and interest groups, not representatives of the larger party constituency.

Critics also look askance at the claim that the present system preserves the sovereignty of the party's rank and file. Increased participation in primaries has come at a cost—in the quality of participation and the representativeness of those who do participate. The extraordinary volatility in support for candidates (between February 25 and March 2, 1984, the percentage of Democrats who preferred Gary Hart for the nomination increased from 7 percent to 34 percent) suggests how little primary voters know about candidates on the ballot and how easily moved they are by media attention and campaign spectacles. And with only about a fourth of the voting age population showing up at the polls, the primary electorate is skewed toward the well-educated, the well-heeled, and the ideologically extreme. Moreover, since the critical choices are usually made in the early state caucuses and primaries, the vast bulk of voters are effectively disfranchised. At best they can register their preferences among a sharply reduced field of candidates.

When these three sets of criticisms of the present nominating system are joined with other widely acknowledged shortcomings—the damage done to the eventual nominee in a highly contested race, the distortion of party platforms and rules by a process dominated by agents of those few candidates who are able to stay the course, the lack of accountability between the nominee and his party—the case against it becomes compelling. Yet to acknowledge these problems is not to embrace alternative arrangements. Moving from diagnosis to treatment is complicated by uncertainty about the connection between means and ends and by conflict over values.

Thinking about Reform

The first complication comes from judging the system by the fruits it has borne. For the Republican party the postreform process has renominated three presidents (two who then won landslide victories in the general election and one who lost by a whisker in the very difficult Watergate era) and produced in the one completely open contest a candidate who subsequently unseated the incumbent and became a highly successful president. The Democratic experience has been almost the reverse. For them the new system produced only one president, and he was judged by many to be ineffective in office, a verdict confirmed by the voters in his unsuccessful reelection drive. Both the other nominees—one on the ideological extreme, the other in the party mainstream—were overwhelmed in the general election.

It is hard to make a case that these divergent experiences stemmed from differences in the Republican and Democratic nomination systems. The parties do differ. The Republicans, unlike the Democrats, have preserved a strong element of local control and discretion: the rules permit state parties wide latitude in delegate selection procedures, allowing states to adapt their processes to local political conditions.[3] The Republicans have also avoided having their rules held hostage to the short-run calculations of presidential candidates, as has occurred in the Democratic party. But the Republicans have not been unscathed by the reforms that swept through the Democratic party. Statutory changes made in response to mandates from the national Democratic party and other societal forces moved the Republican nomination process in a plebiscitary direction—dominated by primaries, open to outsiders, responsive to populist appeals, influenced by the media. Differences in process between the parties cannot account for differences in outcomes.

No set of institutional arrangements for nominating presidents will guarantee good candidates and a bright future for the party. The rules are important, but they operate within a larger context of issues, candidates, party loyalties and images, the record of the administration, the media, interest groups, and public opinion. Weak candidates and ineffective presidents were nominated on occasion under systems dominated by party leaders, and strong candidates and effective presidents can emerge under the reformed process of today. The task of reform is to increase, however marginally, the odds of a favorable outcome—one in which each party produces a strong candidate who, if elected, will make an effective president—and to improve the workings of democratic government.

Disagreement over what constitutes a strong and effective party confounds any easy identification of means.[4] Those attracted to a party regular or elite model prefer to strengthen the role of professional politicians, whose pragmatic orientation toward winning elections leads them to seek candidates who can make centrist appeals and reinforce existing loyalties. Those who favor a reform or participatory model stress the importance of an open process that encourages issue-oriented activists to sharpen differences among candidates and voters to participate directly in the choice of the nominee.

The party-regular school, on one hand, feels most comfortable with the mixed system of prereform days, when state and local party leaders and major interest groups held the balance of power and primaries were used more to test the popular appeal of candidates than to amass a majority of delegates at the national convention. In the present context, this means supporting unpledged delegate status for party and elected officials, wider discretion over delegate selection for state parties, fewer primaries, and a truly deliberative national convention. The reform group, on the other hand, looks favorably on the participatory system that emerged after 1968 and takes special pride in the sharp increase in turnout in presidential primaries. This school tends to oppose special status for party and elected officials and to support national party guarantees of open primaries and caucuses, fair reflection of presidential preferences (proportional representation of primary voters by pledged delegates), and demographic representation of groups.

These competing views of political parties and presidential nominations, though most sharply drawn within the Democratic party, have coincided roughly with ideological divisions within both parties. Democratic party regulars seek to moderate the image of the party and thereby broaden its electoral appeal among blue-collar workers, ethnic groups, and southern whites. Party reformers stress the need to redefine the Democratic coalition and mobilize new voters by staking out new positions on new issues, not by returning to old ones. Among the Republicans, party insurgents, including Ronald Reagan, have found the reformed system hospitable to their moves to redefine and expand the party, while the regulars worry that the New Right agenda and budget deficits will cost the party the support of average Americans. Proposed changes in the presidential nominating system will be judged partly by whether they favor elite or participatory values and partly by which forces within each party are likely to be helped or hurt.

Proposals for Change

Proposals for change can be discussed in three major groups:

- proposals that seek more involvement by party elites, either by providing greater autonomy to state parties or by reserving delegate slots for elected and party officials
- proposals that standardize state delegate selection practices through national party rules or federal statute, including restricted dates for primaries and regional clusters of primaries
- proposals for a one-day national primary, to nominate a presidential candidate directly, to select a nominee from among candidates slated by a party convention, or to select some of the delegates to a party convention

Party Elites. The conversation about the need for more active involvement by party leaders has been conducted almost entirely within the Democratic party. The Democratic National Committee's Commission on Presidential Nomination, chaired by Governor James B. Hunt, Jr., of North Carolina, approved for 1984 two major changes in the rules regulating delegate selection: reserving 568 delegate slots (14.4 percent of the convention) for unpledged party and elected officials and allowing states greater discretion in designing delegate selection systems (and specifically allowing direct elections of delegates at the district level—labeled by critics "loophole" primaries).[5]

Democrats were motivated by several developments. The first was a dramatic decline in the percentage of senators, representatives, and governors attending Democratic national conventions after 1968. The requirement that delegates make an early declaration of preference for a presidential candidate and the necessity of competing with their own constitutents discouraged national politicians from running for convention delegate. The pressure on states to use at-large slots to balance their delegations demographically, moreover, made it unlikely that the predominantly white, male elected officials would be appointed at the state level as delegates. Second, many Democratic party officials were concerned that the use of proportional representation to allocate delegates in primaries devalued the core Democratic constituencies in northern industrial states, many of which had used direct election systems before they were banned by national party rules.

These new rules played a part in Walter Mondale's successful quest for the 1984 Democratic nomination, although his near defeat on "Super Tuesday" dramatizes how the nomination system remains largely unchanged.[6] Moreover, part of the price Mondale paid for a unified convention was the establishment of the new Fairness Commission, with a mandate (though not a formal requirement) to repeal the Hunt reforms. Developments within the Democratic National Committee since the party's devastating defeat in the 1984 election make it likely that the changes sought by Gary Hart and Jesse Jackson will be resisted, but whether the party will move in the direction of greater state party autonomy or a more central role for public officials is problematic.

Republicans see little need for adjusting their rules in a similar fashion, since states already enjoy considerable latitude in selecting delegates. The Republican national party has no rules requiring a declaration by delegates of their candidate preference, proportional representation, equal division between men and women, or affirmative action plans or goals (although party guidelines urge state parties to take positive action to achieve the broadest possible participation in party affairs). Moreover, Republican officeholders have maintained a consistently high level of participation in Republican conventions. Although Republican rules prohibit ex officio delegates, more lenient rules regulating other aspects of the delegate selection process make it relatively easy for party and elected officials to run as delegates and to be appointed by state parties.

Neither of these two features of the Republican nominating process, however, has consistently strengthened mainstream forces in the party. At times state party officials and members of Congress have taken the lead in pushing the party toward its ideological extreme, gambling that a minority party must present a "choice, not an echo" if it is to succeed. Representative Newt Gingrich, who with several House colleagues fought successfully to include in the 1984 platform basic tenets of the "conservative opportunity society," saw this feature as a positive force for the Republican party: "This is a year almost like 1896. The country faces two very radical choices. We are moving toward a consciously polarized election."[7]

The most radical proposal for strengthening the role of party elites in presidential selection is to have Congress require that the nominating convention of each party consist of its elected public officials and party leaders—its senators, representatives, governors, state party chairs and vice chairs, mayors of major cities, and members of the national committees—with no presidential primaries at all. This plan, similar to the system used by many other democratic countries to select their party leaders, puts a premium on peer review and on indirect expressions of popular will. An elite-dominated system of this sort, however, seems ill suited to the antiparty, plebiscitary strains in the American political culture. Most serious proposals for changing the nominating system move in the direction of increasing or channeling, not eliminating, participation by rank-and-file party identifiers.

Standardizing Nominating Procedures. The Democratic party has led the way in seeking to nationalize the delegate selection process, but a good deal of variation remains among states in the kinds of primaries, filing deadlines, allocation of delegates, number of candidates, and the like. Representative Morris Udall, a contender for the 1976 Democratic presidential nomination, was frustrated by the lack of uniform rules and procedures: "A candidate's future is in the hands of a hodgepodge of laws, regulations, and faceless officials over whom he has no control or recourse."[8] Udall and others have proposed a set of changes to standardize the nominating system, particularly the timing of primaries.

Several years ago the Democratic party sought to shorten the nominating system and to reduce the importance of early caucuses and primaries by creating a three-month "window" within which all delegate selection events must be held. In the face of protests from Iowa and New Hampshire, however, the party gave waivers to these two states, thereby leaving the existing system largely intact. The Udall plan allows no such exceptions.[9] It prescribes four dates—the second Tuesday in March, April, May, and June—on which a state must schedule its primary if it chooses to hold one. Under the proposal a full list of candidates, including all who are receiving federal matching funds, must be on the ballots of all states, and every candidate who wins 10 percent or more of the votes in the presidential preference primary must be allocated a proportional share of the delegates. On each of the four dates, primaries would be held in a number of states, in different areas of the nation. The distribution of primaries among the four dates would depend on the individual choices made by the states, but the plan assumes that each date would attract a significant number of diverse states.

The primary advantage of restricting the dates of state primaries is that it may lead to a more deliberative process. Since the official start of the nomination season would include contests in a number of states across the country, no individual candidate would benefit from his or her appeal in a single region or ride an artificial, media-created momentum generated by a favorable showing in a single state. The field of candidates would not narrow so quickly, at least not on the basis of outcomes in only one or two states. The month between primary dates could be used profitably by candidates to present their case and by primary voters to consider the various aspirants. Four Super Tuesdays would probably generate more interest than the present system and produce a larger and more representative turnout. Free media, especially candidate debates, might well become even more important than paid advertising. The process would remain sequential, allowing candidates to be tested over a period of time, but would be less prone to sudden and decisive shifts in public opinion resulting from horse-race coverage.

Critics believe these benefits are problematic and, in any case, achievable only at two substantial costs. First, states would be forced to pay the price of standardization. The dates of many primaries, some of which are rooted in local political traditions, would have to be changed, and states would lose the option of conducting beauty contest or direct election primaries. Some, like New Hampshire, might even resist by holding "unofficial" events before the start of the primary season. Second, the plan would favor well-known, established candidates by eliminating the opportunity for an outsider to emerge from the pack by successfully concentrating resources in a single state. Actually, unknown candidates could still target their resources on an individual state and attempt to make their performance there a publicized test of their popularity. Their victory in one state, however, would be tempered by the results of other primaries from around the country.

A variation on the plan to restrict dates for state primaries is the idea of regional primaries. This plan comes in two versions: the first, similar to the Udall plan, a regional clustering of optional state primaries; the second, more restrictive in scope, compulsory state primaries in regional groups. Under both versions states are allocated among five regions, and the date for each regional primary is determined by lot. The former permits states to retain caucus or convention systems of delegate selection, the latter relies exclusively on primaries, proportional representation, and pledged delegates.

A regional clustering of primaries seems better suited for conserving the energies and funds of candidates than for helping the parties select their best nominees. While the shifting order of primaries from one presidential election year to the next would prevent any long-term influence of early states, the first regional primary in any year could unduly boost a candidate with a largely regional appeal. Time-zone primaries would avoid the most extreme bias of regional primaries, but they too would limit the setting in which candidates are tested in the critical opening of the primary season.

National Primary. The most frequently mentioned proposal for changing the presidential nominating system is the direct national primary. While many variations have been proposed, the most common form calls for Congress to establish a single national primary for each party on a designated date in August. Candidates would qualify by filing petitions with signatures equal to at least 1 percent of the votes cast in the previous presidential election. If no candidate received a majority (40 percent in some plans) of the votes cast in a party's presidential primary, a runoff election would be held several weeks later between the two candidates receiving the most votes. The national party conventions could still be held to select the vice-presidential nominee, adopt the platform, and conduct other party business.

The case for the national primary begins with its simplicity.[10] If the complexity of the present mélange of rules were replaced by a simple, uniform system, the process would become more comprehensible to the average citizen. This, combined with the full slate of candidates, the direct connection between the primary and the selection of the nominee, and the concentrated media attention on the single date, would probably produce a higher turnout and an electorate more representative of rank-and-file identifiers. The special weight enjoyed by states with early primaries would vanish, since votes from around the country would count equally. Without any special advantage accruing to candidates for campaigning in Iowa and New Hampshire a year or more in advance, the disincentives now facing responsible officeholders would diminish, and the pool of political talent from which presidents are selected would thereby be enlarged. While the media would continue to play a critical role (arguably an even more important one) under a national primary, the distorting effects of press interpretations of the early events would be eliminated. All these factors should increase the probability that the nominee is the first choice in the party rank and file.

While the direct national primary is regularly endorsed by large majorities in the Gallup poll, it has been strongly resisted by party activists and analysts, regulars and reformers. Critics see two major drawbacks of the direct national primary. The first is its shortcomings as a system for choosing the best nominee. A national primary would give established, well-known politicians an overwhelming advantage over newer candidates seeking to air issues and identify public concerns not recognized by the party establishment. As a result, the parties would lose an important device for adapting to new currents in the citizenry. A single national primary might lead the parties to select a candidate with ephemeral appeal. The advantage of stringing the decision over several months is that the competition among candidates gives voters an opportunity to unmask unrealistic and demagogic positions and personal failings. Voters would have little opportunity to benefit from judgments made by the candidates' professional peers. Finally, as a device for registering and counting first preferences, the national primary is limited in its ability to discover the candidate with the broadest—as opposed to the most intense—support. Factional candidates disapproved of by a majority of the party's voters could well emerge.

The second argument against the national primary is its likely effect on the party system. Austin Ranney states the argument clearly:

> The parties are very sick now. Some analysts believe their sickness is mortal, and they may be right. But if [compulsory regional primaries or a direct national primary] is adopted, they will surely die. If we stay our hands from delivering the final blow, we at least leave open the possibility that some day they may recover. Believing, as I do, that political parties have been invaluable aggregating, moderating, consensus-building agencies in all democratic politics, especially our own, I can only conclude that dismantling them even

further by a universal federalized primary would be a cost far greater than any benefit or set of benefits such a primary could possibly bring.[11]

These arguments against a direct national primary are powerful but not altogether convincing. Well-known, established politicians ought to be favored over unknown, inexperienced candidates. If an outsider has a compelling case to take to the public, one ignored by well-established figures in the party, nationally televised debates and other free media should provide an opening. Parties that fail to recognize new currents of public opinion when nominating their presidential candidates will eventually learn from the outcome of the general election.

Moreover, although extended public discussion and deliberation on the candidates are desirable, a national primary is no more defective in this regard than the present system. A lengthy and well-publicized campaign before a national primary, especially one featuring televised debates among candidates, provides no less opportunity to scrutinize candidates than a sequential process with a series of outcomes and interpretations. And although peer review would be a highly desirable element, present nominating arrangements provide precious little of it. The public choice problem of aggregating preferences in a multicandidate field is real but as much a factor in the present system as in a national primary.

It is also not obvious that a national primary "would be the final nail in the coffin of the party system." The parties are not major players in the present nominating system; yet in recent years they have adapted to their hostile environment by serving other important functions. National and state party organizations have been strengthened, and the congressional parties have also shown signs of vitality. A similar adaptation might occur in conjunction with a national primary. By divorcing conventions from the nominating process, parties might be able to regain control of their platforms and party rules, now dominated by the candidates, and play a more central role in the general election campaign. A national primary could strengthen the parties by reducing the divisiveness that often follows a series of bitterly fought state primaries and caucuses. It might also dilute the influence of issue groups whose positions are unappreciated by a majority of the party's rank and file.

Party regulars have proposed a variation of this plan in which a one-day national primary is used to select two-thirds of the delegates to a national party convention, the other third having ex officio status by virtue of their position as elected public officials or party leaders.[12] This plan seeks to blend participatory and elite values, rather than choose between them. A candidate who decisively wins the national primary, even though short of the majority of convention delegates, is almost certain to capture the nomination under this arrangement. As Byron Shafer has observed, party and public officeholders are unlikely to upset an emerging consensus on the nominee at the last moment.[13] Such officials could play a decisive role, however, when a national primary produced mixed results. At that point a deliberative convention, weighted with experienced politicians, would be preferable to a runoff election.

Another proposal is to hold a national primary to decide among candidates slated by a national party convention.[14] Delegates to the party conventions would be chosen by caucus or convention systems in each state, with uniform starting dates and rules binding delegates to support their presidential candidates on the first ballot at the national convention. A block of 25 percent of each state's delegation would be officially uncommitted and reserved for elected and party officials. Any candidate who received 70 percent of the national convention vote would automatically be the party's nominee for the general election. Otherwise the top two or three finishers would appear on the ballot in a national primary held in September. The postconvention primary plan, now used to nominate statewide candidates in Colorado and Connecticut, seeks both to revitalize the role of political parties and to accommodate the pressure for plebiscitary devices in presidential selection.

All the proposals for a national primary, as well as most that seek to standardize state delegate selection processes, entail overriding party rules with national legislation. Whether so drastic a solution is necessary or desirable depends on how seriously one views the problems of the current presidential nominating system, how likely a reformed system is to produce better candidates and more effective presidents, and how able the political parties are to adapt and prosper in a federalized presidential selection system.

Conclusion

None of the suggested reforms are likely to achieve the exaggerated claims of their advocates—the revival of the two-party system, the elimination of undue press attention, peer review of prospective candidates. By the same token, critics probably overstate the negative consequences of radical proposals to redefine the institutional arrangements for nominating presidents. The complex forces in our presidential selection system that often overwhelm the designs of reformers can also temper the potentially harmful fallout from major institutional changes. We ought to be open to new arrangements but sober about their likely consequences.

The Democratic party would be well advised to break the cycle whereby presidential candidates manipulate the rules for their own short-term political advantage and struggles over how the nomination contest is waged take precedence over party-building activities. The Republican party's bulwarks against candidate-inspired changes in the rules of the game can serve as a model for the Democrats, as can the Republican norm of local control and discretion.

To the extent that they can avoid the quadrennial spectacle of rewriting their rules and ease the restrictions on state parties, allowing them to adapt their processes to local political conditions, the Democrats will have improved their presidential nominating system.

At least in the short run, however, deregulation of Democratic party rules will do little to alter the basic characteristics of the contemporary presidential selection system. This approach to change is inspired by a belief that natural and healthy processes will evolve gradually after the artificial and unnecessary restrictions have been removed. Those less optimistic about the direction and pace of this development or more impatient about the present system must entertain the more difficult and risky proposals for standardizing nomination procedures or for adopting some form of national primary. Both courses of action are worthy of serious consideration.

Notes

1. These arguments are summarized in William Crotty and John S. Jackson III, *Presidential Primaries and Nominations* (Washington, D.C.: CQ Press, 1985).

2. See Nelson W. Polsby, *Consequences of Party Reform* (New York: Oxford University Press, 1983); and Jeane J. Kirkpatrick et al., *The Presidential Nominating Process: Can It Be Improved?* (Washington, D.C.: American Enterprise Institute, 1980).

3. Robert J. Huckshorn and John F. Bibby, "National Party Rules and Delegate Selection in the Republican Party," *PS* (Fall 1983), pp. 656–66.

4. Crotty and Jackson, *Presidential Primaries and Nominations*, pp. 216–20.

5. David E. Price, *Bringing Back the Parties* (Washington, D.C.: CQ Press, 1984).

6. Thomas E. Mann, "Elected Officials and the Politics of Presidential Selection," in Austin Ranney, ed., *The American Elections of 1984* (Durham, N.C.: Duke University Press, 1985).

7. Quoted in Alan Ehrenhalt, "Reagan-Mondale: A Polarizing Contest," *Congressional Quarterly Weekly Report*, August 24, 1984, p. 2067.

8. Quoted in Crotty and Jackson, *Presidential Primaries and Nominations*, p. 229.

9. The Udall plan and others discussed below are described in Austin Ranney, *The Federalization of Presidential Primaries* (Washington, D.C.: American Enterprise Institute, 1978).

10. Michael Nelson, "Two Cheers for the National Primary," in Thomas E. Cronin, ed., *Rethinking the Presidency* (Boston: Little, Brown, 1982).

11. Ranney, *Federalization of Presidential Primaries*, pp. 35–36.

12. Kirkpatrick et al., *Presidential Nominating Process*, pp. 15–16.

13. Byron E. Shafer, *Quiet Revolution* (New York: Russell Sage Foundation, 1983), p. 537.

14. Thomas Cronin and Robert Loevy, "The Case for a National Pre-primary Convention Plan," *Public Opinion* (December/January 1983), pp. 50–53.

Participants in the Nominating Process: The Role of the Parties

Martin P. Wattenberg

In his famous 1942 book *Party Government*, E.E. Schattschneider wrote that nominations have become "the distinguishing mark of modern political parties; if a party cannot make nominations it ceases to be a party."[1] Today it appears that the presidential nomination process has changed so as to render political parties an endangered institution. While rapid change is relatively common-place in the current political scene, the major transformations in the presidential nomination process over the past two decades are particularly striking. And, as Schattschneider would lead us to expect, no other institutional change has had such a profound effect on the state of our political parties. Parties are in trouble because they have come to be neglected by the voters and politicians alike. Such neglect has been made possible to a large extent by the withering of the party's role in the presidential nomination process.

One of many reasons why political scientists and practitioners value parties is for their important role in clarifying the extraordinarily complicated American political system for the voter. Our system of separate institutions sharing power not only makes the process of policy making long and cum-bersome but also makes it difficult for even the most astute observer to assess who is ultimately responsible for political outputs. The common tie of par-tisanship, however, theoretically links readers from the disparate centers of governmental power in an extraconstitutional yet unmistakable fashion. Be-cause of their common commitment to a comprehensive program for public policy, members of the party in government can be held accountable by the public for the success or failure of the party's program. Thus, with only the knowledge of a candidate's party affiliation, the average voter can easily make an informed choice on the basis of an evaluation of what the party as a whole has proposed and done. This principle of collective responsibility not only simplifies decision making for the electorate but also facilitates cooperation both within and between the various governmental institutions. Elected officials of a party who anticipate that they will experience a common fate at the polls will be much more likely to act in concert.

All of this collapses, however, when politicians are nominated because of their own programmatic views and personal qualifications, without regard to their loyalty or service to the party. Such a process enables them to build their own individual electoral coalitions and frees them from the norms of collective responsibility within their nominal party. Such entrepreneurial behavior no doubt best ensures their continuance in public office. The problem is that it detracts from the coherence and stability of the system by fostering a free-floating politics in which political coalitions have to be continuously built anew and political responsibility is difficult to affix.

Such a phenomenon is clearly apparent in the decline of party voting in the Congress and in the numerous problems presidents have had in obtaining cooperation from their fellow partisans in Congress. Echoing this lack of partisanship among the politicians, the electorate has adjusted its attitudes toward the parties accordingly. For example, a 1973 survey of young adults and their parents found that 92 percent of the young people and 86 percent of their parents agreed with the statement, "A candidate's party label does not really tell a person what the candidate's stand will be on the issues."[2] In 1980 a national survey yielded the following results about Americans' attitudes toward parties:

- 71 percent agreed that "the best rule in voting is to pick a candidate regardless of party label."
- 52 percent agreed that "the parties do more to confuse the issues than to provide a clear choice."
- 45 percent agreed that "it would be better if, in all elections, we put no party labels on the ballot."
- 30 percent agreed that "the truth is we probably don't need political parties in America anymore."

One possible interpretation of all this is that the electorate is disenchanted with Democrats and Republicans alike and views each party negatively. My interpretation, as described at length elsewhere, is quite different.[3] Rather than becoming negative toward the parties, the data shown in table 1 indicate a growing neutrality in public attitudes toward the two parties. Since 1952 the percentage neutral toward both parties has increased from 13.0 to 35.8 percent, whereas the percentage negative toward both has been relatively stable. Virtually all the people who are placed in the "neutral-neutral" category exhibit the following response pattern to the four open-ended questions about the parties upon which table 1 is based:

Q. What do you like about the Democratic party?
A. Nothing.

TABLE 1
THE PUBLIC'S EVALUATIONS OF THE TWO PARTIES, 1952–1984

	Negative Negative	Negative Neutral	Neutral Neutral	Positive Negative	Positive Neutral	Positive Positive
1952	3.6	9.7	13.0	50.1	18.1	5.5
1956	2.9	9.0	15.9	40.0	23.3	8.9
1960	1.9	7.5	16.8	41.4	24.2	8.3
1964	4.4	11.2	20.2	38.4	20.6	5.0
1968	10.0	13.8	17.3	37.5	17.4	4.1
1972	7.9	12.6	29.9	30.3	14.7	4.7
1976	7.5	11.8	31.3	31.1	13.7	4.5
1980	5.0	8.6	36.5	27.3	17.7	4.8
1984	3.0	7.7	35.8	31.3	18.0	4.1

NOTE: The figures on each party are calculated by counting the number of positive responses and subtracting the number of negative responses. A failure to say anything results in 0-0 and is therefore coded as neutral. For further information, see Martin P. Wattenberg, *The Decline of American Political Parties, 1952–1980* (Cambridge, Mass.: Harvard University Press, 1984), chap. 4.
SOURCE: 1952–1984 SRC/CPS University of Michigan National Election Studies.

Q. What do you dislike about the Democratic party?
A. Nothing.

Q. What do you like about the Republican party?
A. Nothing.

Q. What do you dislike about the Republican party?
A. Nothing.

In the 1950s such a response pattern reflected general political ignorance. Most of these people had little to say about the candidates as well and were of little importance, because of their political apathy and consequent low turnout. Today this group is tuned out from the parties but not from the candidates or from politics in general. Indeed, it is often considered the most important group in American electoral politics—known collectively as "the floating voters."

The problem of party decline is therefore one of relevancy more than anything else. Parties will be revitalized only if they can again demonstrate that they perform a useful function in American government—from the recruitment of leaders to the implementation of policies. This paper focuses on the question of recruitment, first addressing what role the changes in the nomination process have played in fostering the irrelevance of our parties, then assessing some of the adjustments to the process in 1984, and finally suggesting some desirable reforms.

The Decline of the Parties' Role in the Nominating Process

Given the importance of the nominating process to political parties, it should not be surprising that many scholars consider the adoption of the direct primary during the progressive era the major cause of the sharp decline of parties that occurred in this early period. Taking the nominating power away from the party machines and giving it to the people was touted as a way to eradicate corruption from the nominating process, but it was also recognized that direct democracy would profoundly weaken the parties.

Fortunately for the parties, the one major political office that largely escaped the reform of the direct primary was the most important, the presidency. Scholars of political parties have labeled the period from the inception of presidential primaries around the turn of the century to 1968 as the "mixed system" of presidential nominations. This refers to the fact that the decision process was a mixture of two elements—the support of party leaders who could deliver large blocks of delegates and popular support as expressed through the primaries. Yet to say that the process was mixed is not to say that it was mixed evenly. The support of the party leaders was clearly paramount.

The major driving force in initiating change in the process, I believe, was the development of television and its coverage of the campaign. Indeed, one cannot address the evolution of the party's role in the nomination process without stressing television's crucial role. Although recent internal party reforms have surely been important in themselves, the most critical factor in determining their effect has been how television coverage of the campaign has changed. No matter how reformers may intend the system to work, it is how the process is covered by the networks that is most consequential. Television coverage of the long-established mixed system played a large part in leading to the reforms after 1968 in the first place, and subsequent coverage of the reformed process has stood some of the reformers best intentions on their heads.

Although primaries were largely important as a way to impress party leaders as late as 1968, television coverage gave voters the impression that their role was much greater. As Richard Rubin notes, by 1968 network coverage was devoted almost entirely to the primaries, even though the majority of the delegates were chosen through caucuses.[4] As a result, a significant gap developed between the public's perception of how the nomination process worked and how it really operated. What people saw on their television screens was a populist process in which winning primaries was essential, whereas what really mattered went on behind the scenes in the traditional manner.

No doubt this contrast contributed heavily to the turmoil on the floor of the 1968 Democratic convention. The antiwar forces felt not only that the rules were manipulated against them in caucuses but also that their primary

50

victories had been overturned. Furthermore, much of the public (having been exposed to the primary process in greater depth than ever before by television) agreed. These forces could do little to stop Humphrey from getting the nomination without having entered a single primary, but they were able to initiate a set of reforms that would soon transform the nomination process.

The reforms established by the McGovern-Fraser commission as well as the consequent changes in state laws affecting the Republican party joined the television version of the campaign to political reality. In itself, this is certainly not undesirable. The problem is that television created a process that is often in direct contrast to what the reformers intended and that many feel has weakened the parties and created one of the least well-organized systems for choosing party leaders in the world.

The reformers intended to create a process wherein each vote would count equally. Yet the principle of one man, one vote hardly extends to a sensible proportion of television coverage per vote. Given the number of delegates allocated to each state, contests in California and New York should be far more important than those in Iowa and New Hampshire. Yet, because Iowa and New Hampshire are the first two states to vote, they receive much more coverage than others despite their small size and unrepresentativeness. As Bruce Morton reported the night of the Iowa caucus on the CBS news, "The campaign is not for delegates, it's for images, for what the rest of the country thinks, and political images are formed in these early tests."[5] An indisputable example of how delegates are secondary to images during this "media-hype" period of the process occurred during the Vermont primary in 1984. Because delegates were chosen separately through caucuses in Vermont, the primary was strictly a "beauty contest"—with no direct bearing on the nomination outcome. Nevertheless, it was a major news story for several nights, and Gary Hart's 70–30 percent victory over Walter Mondale earned him an invaluable live three-and-a-half-minute election night interview with Dan Rather at the top of the CBS evening news.

In addition to creating disproportionalities in state importance, television has overridden the reform of proportional representation within individual contests. Although the Democratic party has formally outlawed the winner-take-all primary, television has effectively restored it by giving virtually all the positive coverage to the victor (or occasionally to a losing candidate who astonishes the press by doing better than expected). The 1984 New Hampshire primary was a classic example of this, with Hart pulling extraordinarily positive coverage and Mondale's campaign placed on the ropes on the basis of a ten-point Hart victory and a projected delegate edge of a mere ten to eight. Such heightened media attention can boost a relatively unknown candidate into the national limelight, as it did Jimmy Carter in 1976, George Bush in 1980, and Gary Hart in 1984. It elevated Hart from the choice of only 2 percent of Democratic voters in a February 16 Gallup poll to the choice of over 30

51

percent in several polls taken soon after his New Hampshire triumph.

In contrast, the also-rans in the field, who often number as many as ten or more, soon find their campaigns struggling in obscurity even though only a small proportion of the party's voters nationwide have had the opportunity to express a preference. The lack of media attention to their campaigns and the label of losers that is pinned on them quickly inhibits their ability to raise the money necessary to run in other states. As Jody Powell has said, "You don't so much beat candidates anymore as you bankrupt them." One result of this is that many candidates drop out of the race quite early, in contrast to the mixed system, in which most went all the way to the convention.

After this early screening stage the television coverage diminishes somewhat, but the general lack of organization in the process remains. For several more months the surviving candidates vie for voter support in contests scheduled in an uncoordinated fashion that forces them to criss-cross from one region of the country to another. The drama of the race for the nomination is played out every week in different settings, with the media continuously keeping tabs on who is gaining and losing momentum in much the same way as the football season is covered.

The strain put on a candidate by this system is arguably more intense than most presidents ever have to face once in office. As a former campaign manager summarized the situation: "The physical, emotional, and energy strain is so staggering that you end up with a person whose emotional and physical level has to be beyond human."[6] The toll all of this takes on a candidate is sufficient to discourage even some with admirable credentials from entering. Ten years ago, for example, Walter Mondale bowed out of the 1976 Democratic race, stating that he found that he did not have "the overwhelming desire to be President which is essential for the kind of campaign that is required."[7] Although Mondale changed his mind about running in 1984, it was clearly not because of any sense that the process had become less wearisome. On at least one occasion during the 1984 campaign, he told reporters that his eyes felt like rocks and he was so tired he had to keep talking to stay awake.

Incumbent senators and governors face the additional cost of having to steal time away from their governmental responsibilities for well over a year to wage a viable campaign. As it stands now, being unemployed is a substantial advantage in seeking the presidential nomination. Candidates such as Jimmy Carter in 1976, Ronald Reagan in 1980, and Walter Mondale in 1984 could afford to devote all their energies to the race, whereas others like Henry Jackson, John Anderson, and Gary Hart could not.

Not only the candidates find this a long and over arduous process—so does the public. In a *USA Today* poll taken in late May 1984, 69 percent of the public agreed that "the entire presidential campaign is too long and should be shortened," and 76 percent agreed that "voters lose interest in the campaign because the candidates have to say the same things over and over."[8] As a result, turnout in the primaries and caucuses is usually low and unrepresentative of the party's rank and file.[9]

The effect of all this on party unity and strength has clearly been deleterious. The long series of primary contests virtually ensures that candidates will continually be arguing against one another and attempting to differentiate themselves, even if they have few policy differences. Nelson Polsby points out, for example, that Henry Jackson and Morris Udall were perceived as polar opposites on domestic policy during the 1976 Democratic campaign although their congressional voting records were quite similar.[10] Thus the public comes to see more conflict within the party than really exists and is led to doubt whether the party label really means anything. It is probably more than a coincidence that the party with the most conflictive nominating campaign has lost the general election in every year since the growth of presidential primaries in 1972. As political scientists studying congressional elections have found, divisive primaries do hurt.[11]

Finally, the new nominating process has also weakened the parties by reducing the nominating conventions to little more than media events. As Ray Lockhart, NBC's vice-president for political programming, said in 1984, "As far as we're concerned this year the conventions are just another story. They're no longer an event."[12] To use Walter Bagehot's terms, the national nominating convention has moved from being an efficient institution to being a dignified institution. The convention is no longer where the nomination is made, any more than the monarchy is where the decisions of governing are made in Britain. Each plays a role only in legitimating choices made by more modern political institutions. They are both longstanding institutions that have been superseded by more modern means of making political decisions.

While such a status might be most fitting for the British monarchy, as Bagehot pointed out over a century ago, it does not suit the American party convention very well. The convention is the party's one chance every four years to show the American public what it stands for and to demonstrate its crucial role in the governmental process. Eliminating political decision making from the conventions has made the public more likely to view the parties with indifference and neglect.

The 1984 Democratic Party Reforms

Many political observers have argued for some time that American political parties could be strengthened by restoring the convention to its former prominence and by giving party officeholders a larger role in the process. In fact, the Democratic party's most recent reform commission, led by Governor Hunt of North Carolina, explicitly adopted such a goal. By allotting 14 percent of the delegate slots to party leaders to go to the convention uncommitted and by reversing the 1980 bound delegate rule, the Hunt commission sought to bring deliberation and party control back into the convention. It is ironic that the concept of guaranteed slots was first proposed after the 1968 Democratic convention to ensure the participation of underrepresented groups such as women, blacks, and young people; by 1980 it was the party leaders who were underrepresented, because of the reluctance of most leaders to be formally committed to a candidate.

Besides adding a deliberative element to the convention, it was thought that greater involvement of party officials would reinstate the principle of peer review and make the question of electability more central in the final decision. Of these three goals, the only one realized in 1984 was that of peer review. Although the superdelegates were technically uncommitted, most came to the convention publicly supporting Mondale. This gave him the needed boost to clinch the nomination, even though he had edged out Hart in the primaries by only 38.6 to 36.2 percent of the popular vote. If the superdelegates had come to the convention truly uncommitted, the convention would have been wide open and would probably have gone beyond one ballot. Thus the addition of the superdelegates actually prevented the convention from being decisive in the process.

One of the arguments for having such an element of peer review in the process was that elected officials would be more likely than candidate-centered "amateur" delegates to take into account the long-term future of the party and would therefore support the most electable candidate. What the 1984 experience demonstrated was that party stalwarts will support the candidate they are best acquainted with regardless of whether that candidate is the most electable. Throughout the 1984 campaign the polls showed Hart rather than Mondale to be the more viable candidate against Reagan. The 1984 National Election Study data for March through June confirm this conclusion, with 39.5 percent of all registered voters preferring Mondale to Reagan and 42.6 percent preferring Hart to Reagan.

The other major change made by the Hunt commission with an eye to reinvigorating the party was to shorten the lengthy nomination process by imposing a three-month window period for primaries and caucuses. This created the much-celebrated phenomenon of front loading, which unless reversed will affect the Republican party as well in 1988. The theory behind this change was that putting so many contests early in the campaign would prevent a dark horse from establishing credibility and enable one of the party veterans to build an insurmountable delegate lead and thereby put a quick and efficacious end to the race.

For a short time after the Iowa caucus, it appeared that this change would have precisely the desired effect. Yet, like many other party reforms in the recent past, this one did not work out quite as planned, because of the media's coverage of the campaign. The media quickly jumped at the Hart campaign as the only alternative to Mondale and, after his victories in New Hampshire, Maine, and Vermont, transferred the banner of front-runner to him within two weeks. Hart himself predicted the general course of events in late 1983— telling a group of supporters, as captured in a PBS documentary, the following:

> You can get awfully famous in this country in seven days. I mean it's phenomenal. It doesn't take much. And name recognition— your polls go up. The pattern is you do better than you are supposed to in the early states; that is reported in the analysis of the caucus and primaries. People then get excited about the campaign, begin to talk about you—you're on TV more, you're in the newspapers more, your name recognition goes up, and money begins to come in.[13]

By the time Super Tuesday (March 13, 1984) arrived, front loading had worked to the advantage of the dark horse in that there had been insufficient time for the momentum to subside and for his record to be closely examined. Were it not for the new elements in 1984 of the AFL-CIO endorsement and the superdelegates, Mondale's campaign would probably have followed in the footsteps of Edmund Muskie's 1972 campaign.

In short, despite the renewed concern for the role of the party in the nomination process, the process still remains at a crisis point of mismanagement. Two areas cry out for continued reform: (1) some method to keep the party's candidates from ripping each other and consequently the party apart during the campaign; and (2) a sensible alternative to the current ad hoc schedule of primaries and caucuses. In the following section, I discuss four reforms that I believe would serve to ameliorate these problems.

Some Proposed Future Reforms

Approval Voting. Approval voting is a mechanism whereby voters can cast votes for as many candidates as they approve of rather than being constrained to vote for only one candidate.[14] This reform is particularly appropriate for a primary election since it explicitly recognizes that voters may find a number of the candidates to their liking. If a party is at all ideologically cohesive, there are bound to be more similarities than differences between the candidates. Yet the single-preference voting system encourages candidates to highlight their differences and thereby makes the party seem less cohesive than it in fact is. One result is that candidates who are the most different are advantaged, because those who are similar are hurt by the inevitability of dividing up the same constituency. Candidates who have benefited from just such an advantage in recent years have been George McGovern in 1972, Jimmy Carter in 1976, and Ronald Reagan in 1980. In 1976, for example, the crowded field of liberal candidates split the large left-wing vote, leaving the more centrist candidate

Carter on top.

Approval voting would eliminate this kind of advantage and ensure that the candidate with the widest range of political support gains the nomination. Candidates would thus have an incentive to appeal to the modal point of the party's ideological distribution. In addition, since the candidates could share votes rather than divide them, they would have less incentive to differentiate themselves artificially or to attack one another vociferously. Thus the party should emerge from an approval voting campaign less divided and with greater ideological cohesion.

Giving the Runner-up First Refusal of the Vice Presidency. Another way the parties might try to legislate a less fractious campaign would be to change the rules so that the runner-up in the presidential balloting receives the right of first refusal of the vice-presidential nomination. Of course there is no way to ensure that this person would accept, but the possibility would have to be taken into account during the primary campaign. Knowing that these leaders might have to coexist peacefully on the same ticket in the fall should make for a less warlike struggle between candidates in the spring. In addition, it should be noted that such a ticket proved successful in both uniting the party and winning in November when it was tried by Kennedy in 1960 and Reagan in 1980. I have little doubt that Mondale's vote in 1984 would have been enhanced substantially with Hart rather than Ferraro on the ticket. It is unlikely that 30 percent of Hart's primary supporters would have voted against a Mondale-Hart ticket, as they did against Mondale-Ferraro. The unseemly specter of interest groups lobbying Mondale for their favorite choice for the second slot would also have been avoided. The practice of giving the presidential nominee carte blanche in selecting a running mate is relatively recent and has not generally served the parties well. Ferraro is only one of several hastily made choices in recent history who proved too politically inexperienced for the job and about whom serious personal questions were raised. Establishing the runner-up practice would surely be preferable for the health of our parties and democracy.

Regional Primaries. Perhaps the most likely to be enacted of the four reforms suggested here is that of regional or time-zone primaries. There is widespread dissatisfaction with the lack of any systematic ordering in the current scheduling of primaries. Grouping all the state primaries into four regional or time-zone ones would impose a more rational structure that would cut down on candidates' traveling time and reduce the number of times that the candidates have to square off against one another. It would also eliminate the possibility that one small, idiosyncratic state, such as Iowa or New Hampshire, would receive disproportionate attention, since its contest would be overshadowed by those of larger states in the same area. The major problem that would still remain, however, is the undue influence of whichever region came first. For example, if the western states were the first to vote, any candidate from California would have a clear advantage in building momentum (assuming that the media did not attack the winner for doing worse than "expected"). Although most of the plans that have been proposed call for the order of the regions to be determined by lot each year, the fact that such influence occurs by chance hardly makes it more palatable. In sum, this plan is preferable to the current hodgepodge of primaries, but many of the major problems with the current system would still remain.

A National Primary with a Preprimary Convention. A preferable (though less politically feasible) plan in my view is that of a national primary to be preceded by a party endorsement convention. The idea of holding a national primary to select party nominees for president has consistently enjoyed popular support. Since Gallup first started to ask about a national primary in 1952, a minimum of 58 percent have supported the idea. In the most recent survey, completed in June 1984, 67 percent were in favor, 21 percent opposed, and 12 percent undecided.

Despite this consistent public support for a national primary, there is virtual unanimity against such a reform among those who have written about the nominating process. Probably the most often used argument against it is that it would further weaken America's political parties by removing the last vestiges of party influence on the nomination process. The answer to this problem lies in a device used for years by state parties—that of the preprimary endorsement convention. Under this proposal the convention, rather than ratifying the front-runner in the popular contests, would perform the crucial function of *creating* the front-runner.

The party could also regain true control of the convention by limiting the delegates to party leaders—something that would be politically feasible under this plan, because the rank and file would have a fair chance to participate and reject the convention's choice in favor of another candidate. This would have the added benefit of fostering a more permanent grass-roots party organization, since there would be space for party members other than the current Democratic superdelegates to be made automatic convention delegates.

Of course the danger is that the party could be embarrassed by the voters' overturning its decision. Such an outcome in states that have preprimary endorsements, however, often acts to redirect a party that has strayed in the wrong direction. Furthermore, a good case can be made for this as the most appropriate role for popular participation in the nomination process. The rank and file *should* have the power to check a party that has become corrupt or indifferent to its concerns; what it should *not* have is the power to control the party directly, as it now has.

Another concern often expressed about any national primary proposal

57

has been that it would even further increase the role of the national press. Although this might well be so, I think it important to note that given a shorter and less open-ended process, the press would have far less discretion in reporting it. Moreover, with the hard news more concentrated, the coverage would be more informative and less interpretive. In particular, the convention rather than the media would be the institution that sorts out the serious contenders from the also-rans. The convention would also provide a chance for a little-known figure to demonstrate support within the party and gain national exposure—a much more eminently sensible way of going about this than courting a few thousand voters in Iowa and New Hampshire.

According to Austin Ranney, the history of party reform in the United States, "can be understood as a three-cornered dispute among purists-for-representativeness, purists-for-direct democracy, and professionals-for-competitiveness."[15] The national primary with a preprimary convention can be seen as a mixed design that allows for elements of each. Advocates of direct democracy undoubtedly would be pleased with moving to a national primary. The higher turnout that a national primary would bring should be welcomed by those concerned with representativeness, and the continued existence of the convention would allow this faction to continue to work for representativeness within the party leadership. Finally, the party professionals should stand to gain greater influence than under the current system with the advent of a preprimary convention under party control.

As the planning for the 1988 nomination begins, we would do well to consider these four proposed reforms as means of revitalizing American political parties.

Notes

1. E. E. Schattschneider, *Party Government* (New York: Farrar and Rinehart, 1942), p. 64.

2. Paul Allen Beck, "The Dealignment Era in America," in Russell J. Dalton, Scott C. Flanagan, and Paul Allen Beck, eds., *Electoral Change in Advanced Industrial Democracies* (Princeton, N.J.: Princeton University Press), p. 262.

3. See Martin P. Wattenberg, *The Decline of American Political Parties, 1952–1980* (Cambridge, Mass.: Harvard University Press, 1984).

4. Richard Rubin, *Press, Party, and Presidency* (New York: Norton, 1981).

5. "CBS Evening News Western Edition," February 27, 1985.

6. Quoted in Elizabeth Drew, "Running," in Peter Woll, ed., *Behind the Scenes in American Government*, 4th ed. (Boston: Little, Brown, 1983).

7. Quoted ibid., p. 24.

8. Louis Peck, "Voters Say Campaign Lasts Too Long," *USA Today*, June 6, 1984.

9. See James I. Lengle, *Representation and Presidential Primaries: The Democratic Party in the Post-Reform Era* (Westport, Conn.: Greenwood Press, 1981).

10. Nelson W. Polsby, *Consequences of Party Reform* (New York: Oxford University Press, 1983), pp. 149, 256.

11. See Robert A. Bernstein, "Divisive Primaries Do Hurt: U.S. Senate Races, 1956–1972," *American Political Science Review*, vol. 71 (1977), pp. 540–45.

12. Quoted in Barbara Matusow, "TV Pulling Back from Its Immersion in Party Conventions," *Los Angeles Times*, July 16, 1984.

13. "So You Want to Be President," Public Broadcasting Service documentary.

14. See Steven J. Brams and Peter C. Fishburn, *Approval Voting* (Boston: Birkhauser, 1983).

15. Austin Ranney, *Curing the Mischiefs of Faction: Party Reform in America* (Berkeley: University of California Press, 1975), p. 242.

59

Participants in the Nominating Process: The Voters, the Political Activists

Warren E. Miller

The nominating process has many consequences. I will not attempt an exhaustive listing, but three functions of the process should be noted. The manifest and most visible function is to enable voters to evaluate and choose presidential candidates to represent the political parties. A second function, which follows from the basic nature of our political system, is to provide a focus for the competition for party leadership. A third function, much less visible than the other two though of major importance to the continuity of national politics, is to mobilize political activists, who are influential participants in many arenas of national politics. I want to address two of these functions: the nominating process as an exercise in adult education, and the nominating process as a means of selecting the national presidential campaign elite.

The first topic remains dear to my heart despite the repeated and sometimes justified complaints about the nominating process. For years I was steadfast in defending the process and in arguing the longer the better, whatever the cost to the participants. The origin of that argument lies in the recognition that the health of a democratic society depends in measure on the involvement, the information, and the sophistication of the mass participants. Because our biennial studies give us a rather dismal view of the amount of attention and the amount of information used by the governed to govern themselves, I have argued that anything we can do to enhance the ordinary citizens' familiarity with the candidates will improve the performance of voters in the presidential selection process.

The first report that I want to give stems from a research project that a colleague, Professor Merrill Shanks of the University of California, Berkeley, and I have completed, based on the 1984 National Election Study (Center for Political Studies, Institute for Social Research, University of Michigan). In that study we attempted to monitor the response of the national electorate through time as citizens were exposed to the sequence of national primaries.

Given my commitment to the primaries, I expected to find, across the months, the changes that theories of communication lead us to expect: increased information; increased interest; greater awareness of the candidates' positions on matters of national policy; and greater awareness of the candidates as potential occupants of the White House. I was dismayed to discover that although some of my expectations were realized, they seem to have been fulfilled only up through Super Tuesday, which was only March 13, very early in the primary season.

Looking at the Democratic primaries exclusively, because there was no Republican contest in 1984, we found a growth of recognition of the major contenders. Gary Hart did begin as a virtual unknown, we found, but information about him spread rapidly. More and more people recognized his name, were able to evaluate him as a candidate, and had a sense of where he stood on the issues. All the good things that were supposed to happen, happened.

That happening peaked on Super Tuesday or immediately thereafter. The rest of the primary campaigns brought virtually no growth in knowledge or sophistication or in understanding and appreciation of the contending candidates or their policy positions.

This is not to say that the remainder of the period preceding the nominating conventions was uninteresting; for during that time a series of dramatic changes took place in popular preferences for the two leading Democratic candidates, Vice President Walter Mondale and Senator Hart. In the absence of change in the extent to which people assigned desirable traits to one candidate or the other, what was the source of this dynamic movement within the body politic? Professor Shanks and I think we have located the source. The primary electorate engages in a quite sophisticated form of strategic choice. The choice is related to perceptions of the chances of each prospective candidate in the electoral contest. First is the chance for nomination and ultimately the chance for election—electability in the forthcoming November contest.

As you would expect, voters want to see the man they prefer emerge as a winner, but they also tend to prefer the man who is more likely to win. Voters often deviated from supporting their personal preferences because of altered perceptions about who was likely to be a winner. As the primary and caucus campaigns unfolded, later preferences were indeed a sharp reflection of perceived electability, the second of our factors. The changes in preference had nothing to do, as far as we can tell at this early point in analyzing our 1984 data, with anything other than those strategic perceptions of chances for victory.

Our colleagues who emphasize rational choice will undoubtedly applaud our discovery that voters were behaving quite rationally. They preferred the man they liked best, unless somebody else seemed to have a better chance of being nominated and elected. There is also the possibility that what we were observing was no more than public response to the media presentation

61

of the horse race. In sum, our 1984 primary study leads us to conclude that the continuing series of primaries is not a very successful exercise in preparing the national electorate to participate in the selection of presidential candidates and in the choice of a president. I am left with a sense that the amounts of effort, time, and money that go into the primary elections may bring many results, but the result of improving the quality of mass participation, so essential to an effective plebiscitary democracy, is largely missing.

The Political Activists

Let me turn now to that second function, the mobilization of political activists. The analysis that follows concentrates attention on the political activists whom Jeane Kirkpatrick so aptly named "the presidential elite."[1]

We are now in the second decade of dramatic change in the presidential selection process. Many of the changes are visible because they are the consequences of deliberate alterations in the national framework that governs the process. A full review of the presidential selection process should include an examination of the presidential elite and the changes that have occurred there. It must be recognized that presidential politics in the modern era is still shaped by the perspectives, values, and decisions of tens of thousands of individuals who constitute the political activists of presidential politics, a group that is crucial in linking candidates and party activities to the rank-and-file citizenry. It is this stratum that I have chosen to bring to your attention.

It consists of those individuals from city, district, county, or state who campaign on behalf of presidential candidates. They may or may not be co-opted by the campaign organization as local organizers. They are on the lists, or provide lists, of party workers who staff the party organizations and do the work of the party. They are the financial contributors and the local opinion leaders, who control the early success or failure of candidates and save presidential politics from becoming the complete creature of the mass media and their interpretations. For the most part they are self-chosen political activists who have made personal decisions to become engaged in presidential campaigns. Their decision to become active and participate is not contingent on any formal organizational status. Thus a subsequent decision to withdraw from presidential politics or simply to sit out a campaign can also be taken with no necessary consequences for any formal relationship with party or with other political offices.

Although it is difficult to conceive of a presidential primary or election without them, it is only fair to make clear that we cannot actually measure how crucial they are to fund-raising drives, to the canvassing of voters, or to the processes that, by word of mouth, create the credibility of candidates. Because they play a crucial role in defining the candidacies that are offered to the voters in primary elections, caucuses, conventions, and ultimately the general election campaign, they become a key to understanding the entire presidential selection process. A better description of them will add to our understanding and appraisal of that process.

To overcome the vexing problems of delimiting and defining who these people are, my colleague Kent Jennings and I, like Jeane Kirkpatrick and others, have adopted the tack of defining the presidential activists as people who have, at one time or another, been convention delegates and who have also participated in presidential campaigns beyond the confines of the national convention. The set of political activists that I shall describe in this paper consists of all individuals who were delegates to the Democratic or Republican national conventions in 1972, 1976, or 1980. They are represented by the 50 percent of those delegates who responded to requests for information by filling out self-administered questionnaires and returning them to us after the 1980 elections. Virtually without exception, all these delegates were in fact active campaign participants at least during the year that they were delegates to the convention.

Continuity in Presidential Politics

It is also true, however, that many of them became active in presidential politics well before they became formal delegates, and many of them remained active in presidential politics though no longer serving as delegates to their party conventions. Indeed, given our current tendency to focus on turnover in party leadership as evidence of a party system in disarray, we should note that these activists reflect more continuity in the presidential selection process than we are accustomed to presuming.

When one moves from a focus on the changing roster of presidential aspirants or the changes in convention delegates to the consideration of campaign participation, one becomes impressed with the continuity that is the hallmark of involvement in presidential politics. Beyond this generalization it is also true that there are differences between the Democratic and Republican parties that reflect what we would expect to find for the years of reform from 1972 to 1980. More Democratic than Republican delegates dropped out of participation as active campaigners during that period. Similarly, more Democrats than Republicans were recruited or mobilized themselves on behalf of presidential aspirants. But this is only one source of change that characterizes the presidential elites of the two parties.

A second source of change lies with continuous participants who alter their preferences for candidates as well as their perspectives on the central goals and stated issues of presidential politics. We will from time to time take account of changes in the national parties that stem from such changes within continuing individuals, as well as those that result from turnover in the circulation of persons into and out of the presidential campaign elite.

Social Composition and Support for Party

Turnover in campaign elite personnel has been greater in the Democratic party. Turnover has captured some of the changes in party norms that have been introduced in the deliberate attempts to alter the institutional context of the process of presidential selection. The largest changes occurred between 1968 and 1972 although, at least for women, the requirements for enhanced numerical representation reached their peak in 1980. Until the 1984 convention Republican efforts to broaden the participation of women and minorities were much less visible.

Within the Democratic party the changes in rules for group representation at the conventions did not simply alter the institutional context for delegate selection; they reflected a pervasive alteration in the informal norms that encourage participation. The consequences are well represented by data pertaining to the participation of women through their voluntary decisions to join with, or disengage from, the presidential elite. As table 1 suggests, after the 1972 election women were less inclined than men to drop out of Democratic presidential politics. Moreover, they were visibly more likely than men to take the initiative and engage in presidential campaigning after 1972.

That formal changes in the representation of women as delegates need not extend beyond the nominal activities of the convention is suggested by the corresponding data for Republican activists. In contrast to their Democratic counterparts, Republican women were more likely to disengage after the 1972 convention. Further, they were strikingly less likely, rather than more likely, than men to be mobilized for the 1976 or 1980 campaigns.

These patterns of intraparty as well as interparty differences appear, though somewhat less dramatically, in the representation of minorities among the campaign activists. By 1980 both wings of the Democratic party attracted more women and minority activists than at the time of the McGovern campaign in 1972. In the Republican party, however, despite larger representations of women and blacks in the 1980 convention, the number of women declined among the activists, who were dominated even more by white males than they had been eight years earlier. The basic point is, of course, that norms set in the limited context of how delegates are selected may affect the campaign and the personification of party faction through the body of campaign activists.

After the Democratic party's efforts to broaden the participation base, one of its major concerns was that these efforts would dilute delegates' loyalty to the party. The evidence eight years later suggests that such fears were not well founded. Table 2 shows that the Democrats mobilized after 1972 were as likely to see themselves as strong supporters of their party as their counterparts in the Republican party. This is a cogent comparison, given the general strength of Republican loyalty. The full array of data in table 2, however, makes at least two additional points. The first and most dramatic is that

TABLE 1

PRESENCE OF WOMEN IN CAMPAIGN ELITES, 1972–1980

(percent)

	Participants in Both Years	Disengaged after 1972	Mobilized after 1972
Republicans			
Moderates	39 (419)	48 (75)	28 (76)
Conservatives	34 (674)	37 (71)	27 (134)
Total	36 (1,136)	44 (160)	27 (219)
Democrats			
Liberals	53 (625)	46 (283)	65 (97)
Traditionalists	39 (723)	36 (142)	49 (250)
Total	45 (1,573)	44 (481)	53 (460)

NOTE: Each entry is the proportion of women within the category; for example, of all liberal Democrats who were campaign participants in 1972 and 1980, some 53 percent were women. Figures in parentheses are weighted numbers of cases on which the proportions in this table are based. Party factions are defined by the delegates' reports of their history of preferences for nomination. Democratic liberals report preferences associated with the McGovern-Udall-Kennedy wing of the party; traditionalists' preferences include the Humphrey-Jackson lineage. Republican conservatives preferred Reagan, both in 1976 and 1980; moderates were the supporters of the Ford-Baker-Bush sequence.

TABLE 2

STRONG PARTY SUPPORT AND THE CIRCULATION OF CAMPAIGN ELITES
WITHIN MAJOR PARTY FACTIONS, 1972–1980

(percent)

	1972 Continuously Active	1976 Continuously Active	1980 Continuously Active	1972 Disengaged	1980 Mobilized
Republicans					
Moderates	58 (172)	51 (135)	65 (75)	33 (52)	45 (49)
Conservatives	61 (162)	64 (239)	64 (276)	48 (21)	47 (102)
Democrats					
Liberals	40 (168)	49 (171)	54 (176)	21 (121)	41 (84)
Traditionalists	57 (152)	47 (217)	68 (301)	20 (69)	50 (125)

NOTE: The entries are the percentage of each category describing themselves as strong party supporters. The figures in parentheses are the number of cases in the categories.

factions may differ markedly in attachment to party. The second point is that the passage of time and the addition of successive cohorts of delegates may reduce such differences, both among factions and between parties. The change between 1972 and 1980 gives evidence of this. Although members of both party factions were continuously active in campaigning across the eight-year span, in 1981 the McGovernite delegates were far less likely than the party centrists to call themselves strong party supporters. Moreover, other analyses suggest that the discrepancy was even more dramatic eight years earlier, as Jeane Kirkpatrick reported.[2]

It also appears that the relatively limited support for party by the left wing of the Democratic party contrasted sharply with the partisanship of the right wing of the Republican party. If both groups represent insurgency, with the Democratic liberals challenging the traditional centrist leadership and the Republican conservatives in fact dominating the previously ascendant moderate leadership, then it is clear that transitions in party leadership do not necessarily produce a weakening of the activists' links to the symbol of party.

Campaign Elite Representation of Citizens' Preferences

Although the sources of dissatisfaction with changes in the presidential selection process have been numerous, one consequence of the 1972 experience in the Democratic party bears a singular responsibility for the sense that the presidential election has gone awry. That consequence was reported by Jeane Kirkpatrick in her study of the 1972 convention delegates, based on our extensive analysis of the 1972 convention delegates.[3] It concerns the level of policy agreement between convention delegates and their rank-and-file party supporters. Kirkpatrick noted that the Democratic convention delegates who nominated George McGovern were less in tune with the national policy preferences of Democratic party identifiers than were the Republican convention delegates who nominated Richard Nixon. The conclusion was that the dominant wing of the Democratic party elite did not represent its constituency's preferences, which were, ironically, being better represented by the opposition elite.

Although, as I will note in a moment, the startling evidence of an aberrant Democratic left in 1972 can be replicated in 1980, turnover of personnel in the campaign elites in both parties and changes in the individual activists' opinions produced a quite different configuration of representation relationships in the latter year. The broadest overview is presented in table 3. Entries there reflect varying degrees of similarity and difference between selected sets of delegates and citizens. A comparison of entries in the first two columns reveals that in 1980, in clear contrast to 1972, Democratic activists enjoyed closer agreement with Democratic identifiers across the country than Republican activists did with their rank-and-file constituents. Indeed, a comparison

TABLE 3

DIFFERENCES BETWEEN CONVENTION DELEGATES AND PARTY IDENTIFIERS,
BY PARTISAN COMBINATIONS, 1972 AND 1980

	Democratic Delegates/ Democratic Identifiers	Republican Delegates/ Republican Identifiers		Democratic Delegates/ Republican Identifiers		Republican Delegates/ Democratic Identifiers
Issue index	.29	.38	<	.43	<	.57
Group evaluation index	.32	.53	=	.51	<	.73
Liberal or conservative self-placement	.25	.20	<	.53	=	.56

NOTE: Entries are product-moment correlations (r) and indicate the relation between party status (identifiers versus delegates) and attitude. The higher the score, the greater the difference between delegates and identifiers.

of the entries in columns two and three makes the point that the congruence between the Republican elite and mass was in fact markedly greater than the agreement between Democratic delegates and Republican identifiers on only one of the three indicators available to us. In essence, however, the system was working about as it should to provide elite representation of mass preferences in 1980, because the activists of each party represented their own constituents more than they represented the constituents of the opposing party. This is shown in columns three and four.

For a different perspective, note that turnover in campaign elite personnel has tended to lower the level of representation and to highlight the discrepancies between the continuously active elites and their partisan followers. In 1981 the continuously active members of the campaign elites were more distant from their own identifiers in 1980 than were either those who had disengaged from active participation after 1972 or those who were subsequently mobilized into the ranks of the active. The explanations for this apparently perverse pattern are complex and too intricate to recount here.[4] It is evident from our research that turnover in elite campaign personnel can alter the extent to which campaign activists represent the party's followers. In the period under observation, mobilization ''worked'' as democratic theory would have it, bringing into the party elites those new activists who were in closer rapport with party followers. At the same time, factors responsible for disengagement caused both elites to lose former activists who were in closer rapport with party identifiers across the nation than the activists who remained engaged in the 1980 presidential campaign.

A slightly more elaborate sorting of activist factions into genealogies of candidate preferences reveals some rather astounding differences within both

67

parties. Our data, in table 4, provide evidence that in 1981 the Reagan supporters stood in sharp contrast to the activists representing the Ford-Bush legacy. The latter were in substantial agreement with Republican party identifiers across the nation, while the conservative Reagan activists stood in marked disagreement and reflected large differences of issue preferences and ideological evaluations from those of the Republican rank and file.

The data for the Democratic activists bring us full circle. Note in table 5 that the consistent liberals (a subset of the McGovernites from 1972) were as estranged from the rank-and-file Democrats in 1981 as the Reagan supporters were from rank-and-file Republicans. Ironically, the set of Democratic activists who demonstrated greatest rapport with their national constituency were those centrists who had moved to a preference for Carter in 1976 or the newly mobilized who came into presidential politics in 1976 or 1980 on behalf of Carter.

Insofar as representation of rank-and-file values and preferences by the elite participants in presidential politics provides a basis for evaluating the nominating process, the picture of 1980 is filled with ironies and paradoxes. The two groups of activists who best represented their parties' national constituencies were those who backed unsuccessful candidates in the contest for the Republican party leadership and those who supported a first-term Democratic president who was unable to secure reelection. The estrangement of the left wing of the Democratic party from its national constituency was matched in 1980 by the disparity between Republican identifiers across the nation and the Republicans who ultimately secured Reagan's nomination.

With the representation of national constituencies as the focus for this analysis, it becomes clear that recent outcomes were only to a minor degree a response to changing rules of the game of presidential selection. Although those changes in the name of reform may have altered the identity of those who succeeded in the competitions for the party leadership and the nomination, it was the ideological preferences associated with enduring party factions that did the most to shape the contours of representation.

Conclusions and Consequences

From our analysis of perceptions that voters acquired and accumulated in early 1984, we conclude that the Democratic primaries provided the means of informing the party faithful and enabling them to develop choices among party candidates for president—up to a certain point. That point was Super Tuesday, March 13. Then, with most of the primaries still to be held and with Final Tuesday, June 5, almost three months away, the information and education function, the first of the two functions I analyzed, gave way to preferences that voters based on a presidential candidate's viability for nomination and later electability. This dramatic change must acquire significance

TABLE 4

DIFFERENCES BETWEEN REPUBLICAN ACTIVISTS
AND REPUBLICAN PARTY IDENTIFIERS,
BY DELEGATES' CANDIDATE SUPPORT HISTORIES, 1981

	Consistent Moderates	Mixed Preferences	Consistent Conservatives
Issue index	.08*	.32	.58
Group index	.26	.52	.76
Liberal or conservative self-placement	−.15	.10	.44

NOTE: Entries are product-moment correlations. The larger the coefficient, the larger the delegate/identifier differences.

TABLE 5

DIFFERENCES BETWEEN DEMOCRATIC ACTIVISTS
AND DEMOCRATIC PARTY IDENTIFIERS,
BY DELEGATES' CANDIDATE SUPPORT HISTORIES, 1981

	Consistent Liberals	Mixed Liberals	Wavering Liberals	Traditional before Carter	Carterites and Disaffected
Issue index	.59*	.48	.36	.14	.06
Group index	.69	.53	.46	.13	.07
Liberal or conservative self-placement	.58	.47	.38	.10	.06

NOTE: Entries are product-moment correlations. The larger the coefficient, the larger the delegate/identifier differences.

as we review the primaries and other components of the prenomination process.

We need also to be aware of the effects of the nomination processes and any change in them on the campaign elites—the troops who join battle in the struggle for the presidency. Between 1972 and 1980 the Republican presidential campaign elite became increasingly a white male preserve. The Republican activists maintained their strong representation of formal positions of power in both party and public office. Although political circumstances led to a decreased emphasis on party in the presidential campaign of 1980, there was no diminution of individual commitment to supporting the party. There was some small increase in emphasis on the importance of issues, and there was a substantial increase in preoccupation with the party's candidate.

As a result of the circulation of personnel into and out of the Republican campaign elite, activists' links with the national rank-and-file Republican constituents were dramatically weakened. The activists moved to support the ideological preferences of a new conservative leadership, while rank-and-file ideological preferences remained largely unchanged.

During the same eight years the Democratic campaign elite broadened its social base to include more representatives of categories that had presumably been excluded from the formal presidential selection process in earlier years. This change in composition was accomplished while maintaining virtual equity with the Republican elite in representing positions of political power, both party and public. Moreover, the turnover in the personnel constituting the Democratic presidential elite clearly strengthened individual commitments to party support. Changes within the cadre of Democratic activists decreased the centrality of candidates and dramatically decreased the salience of issues in the 1980 campaign. These changes were accompanied by a strengthening of the bonds of agreement between Democratic mass preferences and the ideological commitment of the elite.

During the eight years of transition in leadership in both parties, the two party elites sharpened their differences on questions of policy and ideology. Along with increased party regularity in congressional roll-call voting, these sharpened differences presented the national electorate with an increasingly clear set of alternatives to guide their decisions at the polls. Indeed, between 1972 and 1980 the party elites seemed to be striving to approximate the model of responsible party government so long advocated by many political scientists.

During these years the Republicans overcame the handicap of a failed Nixon presidency. By 1980 they had elected a president who was subsequently successful, whether gauged by reelection margins, by the public esteem that he enjoyed well into his second term, or by his ability to recast the role of government. The Democratic party maintained its national electoral visibility both in Congress and in state governments across the nation but failed in the search for viable party and national leadership. Yet, though given little immediate credit, the party reestablished its rapport with the policy preferences of its national constituency. The external reforms in the presidential selection process, symbolized by the increased role of presidential parties, have clearly been very important. However, the ongoing internal contests for leadership within the two parties, and the natural processes of change in the composition of the party elites and the orientations of their members, are equally if not more important as the source of changes that determine the vitality and continued viability of presidential politics.[5]

The natural processes involved in the struggle for power and the adjustments to circumstances made by the political elite within both parties are the central elements of continuity and change within presidential nominating politics.

Notes

1. Jeane Kirkpatrick, *The New Presidential Elite* (New York: Russell Sage, 1976), pp. 268–69.

2. Ibid.

3. Ibid.

4. This paper is based on a larger enterprise carried out by the author and M. Kent Jennings with the valuable assistance of Barbara Farah and Deborah Dodson. Extensive supporting data will appear in a book by Miller and Jennings tentatively entitled *Party Leadership in Transition*.

5. For another comment on these and other constraints on reform, see Austin Ranney, *Curing the Mischiefs of Faction* (Berkeley: University of California Press, 1975), particularly chap. 6.

You Get What You Pay for, but Is That What You Want?

Michael J. Malbin

There is a basic mismatch in presidential nominations between the campaign finance laws and just about everything else in the system. This paper is about how contribution and spending limits have helped to create that mismatch and what might be done about it.

Let me begin by setting some boundaries. First, I shall not be discussing all aspects of campaign finance. Disclosure, income tax checkoffs and credits, postal subsidies, and hundreds of more technical issues could easily fill our time. I pass over them not to denigrate their importance but to focus on what I consider to be a fundamental flaw in the nominating process.

Second, I shall be talking about presidential nominations, not House races, Senate races, or general election campaigns for the presidency. This point may seem obvious but has to be made. Different offices and different phases of the campaign each pose their own problems. To assume that the same rules would have the same effects across the board would be a gross error. To take one example, spending limits are bound to have less effect on the two major parties' presidential candidates—who are offered free network prime time for debates and a story on every nightly news show—than on a congressional challenger whose campaign has to compete for the slightest attention. Presidential primary candidates fall somewhere between these poles. They need to be considered separately. With these two boundaries drawn, let us begin.

Contribution Limits

In 1974 Congress placed a $1,000 limit on personal contributions and a $5,000 limit on contributions from political action committees (PACs). Since then Congress has let inflation erode the real value of this originally low base. The result has been to lengthen the time it takes candidates to build up a network of contributors.

A large network of small contributors is essential for candidates who survive the Iowa caucuses and the New Hampshire primary. At that stage of the campaign, most candidates will have exhausted their available cash. "Momentum"—positive publicity—is one key ingredient in moving forward after the first round, but equally essential is having the ability to cash in on momentum. Before the campaign finance law, candidates might have asked a few contributors with deep pockets to help pay for some last-minute advertising time in a crucial primary. Nowadays those frantic appeals more often than not have to wait for the mails. Raising money quickly in March, April, and May usually means asking for $100 to $1,000 from people who have already given to you or who normally give to other political campaigns. In other words, it means building a "house list" for each campaign. That takes time.

Many presidential candidates even work on their contributors' lists for three years, forming a PAC before the midterm congressional election preceding the first primary. Candidates do not use campaign committees for the whole time, instead of starting with PACs, for two reasons. First, the candidates can ask supporters to give as much as $5,000 per calendar year to the PAC for two years as well as the maximum $1,000 to the campaign committee. Second, contributions given to a presidential campaign committee are not eligible for matching public funds unless they are given after January 1 of the year before the primaries.

Who benefits from the long campaigns imposed by contribution limits? Long campaigns clearly give a major boost to politicians who are out of office. Candidate PACs also permit some senators and House members to compete effectively, if they can take extended leaves from Washington. But it would be wrong to say that current members of Congress were *helped* by the law, in the way former officeholders were: members who can get away from Washington have been doing well ever since the growth of primaries.

Two kinds of politicians clearly were harmed by contribution limits: active congressional committee or floor leaders and sitting governors. Ambitious members of Congress have known, at least since John Kennedy defeated Lyndon Johnson for the 1960 Democratic presidential nomination, that the skills needed to lead a congressional party or committee have little to do with becoming president. Contribution limits did not create the problem but did exacerbate it. The large number of primaries, proportional delegate selection rules, a front-loading primary calendar, and contribution limits all work together to lead presidential candidates from Congress to be part-time legislators for a full two-year congressional cycle. The members most affected are also the ones who are most important for their leadership inside Congress. Whatever this may mean for presidential nominations, the situation harms Congress and therefore harms government.

The same considerations that force most candidates to raise money early also make it hard for anyone to jump into the race late. Robert Kennedy could wait until after the New Hampshire primary before deciding to run in 1968; without a $1,000 limit he was able to raise money quickly from large contributors and creditors for the next primaries. Contribution limits make late entries more difficult; they do not by themselves make such campaigns impossible. Governor Edmund G. (Jerry) Brown, Jr., of California showed in 1976 that a late entrant could still do well under the new finance rules. What really kill this sort of a candidate are front-loaded or proportional delegate selection processes.

Finally, contribution limits stimulate candidates and supporters to look for ways around the limits. Expenditure limits have a similar effect. Because of its importance, I shall treat the subject of getting around the limits separately.

Money and Timing

Contribution limits force candidates to raise money early. Candidates are also spending more money early, partly because it costs money to raise money and partly because of the increased importance of early primaries. Table 1 shows what major presidential candidates spent through their own candidate committees in the year before each set of primaries. The numbers are the percentages of the allowable spending limit for that election's full primary season.

The table shows that 1976 was the last election conducted according to prefinance-limit calendars. Public financing was in effect, but candidates had not yet adjusted themselves to it. Two major changes were obvious by January 1980. In addition to forming candidate PACs, which no one used before 1976, most candidates were spending more of their own campaign's money in 1979 than all but the top spenders of 1975.

Now let us look at early spending in another way. Instead of taking spending as a percentage of the allowable national spending limit, look at what the leading candidates spent through March 31—that is, through the early primaries—as a percentage of each candidate's own total spending through the convention (table 2).

We see in this table, as in the previous table, that 1980 and 1984 were different from 1976. The reason this time, however, has to do more with delegate selection rules and primary dates than with the campaign finance laws. Table 3 shows the percentage of Democratic primary delegates chosen by the end of March and by mid-April in elections since 1968. Republican numbers would show the same basic pattern.

If delegate selection is accelerated, so must a candidate's actions be. In fact, most of the candidates spent their money much more quickly, proportionally, than delegates were chosen. Hart and Mondale spent 64 and 71 percent of their total funds by the end of March; only half the Democratic delegates were chosen by the second Tuesday in April (April 8). Similar

74

TABLE 1

SPENDING BY CANDIDATES, YEAR BEFORE ELECTION, 1975–1983

(percentage of spending limit)

1975 (1976 limit: $10.1 million)			
Democrats		Eugene McCarthy[a]	1
Birch Bayh	3	Milton Shapp[a]	1
Lloyd Bentsen[a]	3	R. Sargent Shriver[a]	2
Edmund G. Brown, Jr.	0	Morris Udall	5
Robert C. Byrd	1	George Wallace	14
Jimmy Carter	6		
Frank Church	1	Republicans	
Fred Harris	3	Gerald Ford	6
Henry Jackson	11	Ronald Reagan	6
1979 (1980 limit: $14.7 million)			
Democrats		George Bush	18
Edmund G. Brown, Jr.	4	Philip Crane	17
Jimmy Carter	19	John Connally[b]	39
Edward Kennedy	15	Robert Dole	4
		Ronald Reagan	34
Republicans		Lowell Weicker	1
John Anderson	3		
Howard Baker	10		
1983 (1984 limit: $20.2 million)			
Democrats		Jesse Jackson	1
Reubin Askew	9	George McGovern	1
Alan Cranston	13	Walter Mondale	27
John Glenn	16		
Gary Hart	7	Republicans	
Ernest Hollings	7	Ronald Reagan	4

NOTE: Percentages are based on the amount reported by the candidates as counting against the expenditure limits.
[a] Amount includes all spending. Candidate did not separate spending subject to the limits.
[b] Connally did not accept public funds and therefore was not subject to the limit.
SOURCE: Compiled from Federal Election Commission reports.

patterns hold for most of the other candidates listed in table 2.[1]

What is going on here is that candidates spend almost everything they have in the early primaries and caucuses. Front-runners try to score an early win; dark horses hope to achieve a breakthrough. Afterward all the candidates have to scramble to raise new money for the later states. The new money never does come in fast enough to keep spending remotely up to the earlier amounts per voter. If the front-runner does not win early, if the dark horse

TABLE 2
PERCENTAGE OF SPENDING THROUGH AUGUST SPENT BY MARCH 31
1976–1984

		1976		
Gerald Ford	43	Jimmy Carter	29
Ronald Reagan	45		
		1980		
George Bush	72	Jimmy Carter	67
Ronald Reagan	75	Edward Kennedy	62
		1984		
Ronald Reagan	23	Gary Hart	64
		Jesse Jackson	31
		Walter Mondale	71

SOURCE: Compiled from Federal Election Commission reports.

TABLE 3
PERCENTAGE OF ALL DEMOCRATIC PRIMARY DELEGATES CHOSEN BY
WEEK OF PRIMARY, 1968–1984

Selected by	1968	1972	1976	1980	1984
Fourth Tuesday in March	2	13	19	38	32
Second Tuesday in April	7	17	33	44	52

SOURCE: David E. Price, *Bringing Back the Parties* (Washington, D.C.: CQ Press, 1984), p. 225, for 1968–1980; 1984 calculated by the author.

does break through, the candidates can only hope that free media coverage of the narrowed field will help make up for a lack of advertising funds.

What this means for the later states can be seen by looking at the full primary season. Table 4 shows spending allocated by the 1984 Democratic candidates to the various states as a percentage of the legal spending limit for each state.[2]

The table shows, most obviously, that all candidates spent a great deal less in most caucus states after Iowa and Maine than in primaries. In primary states Mondale spent a great deal of money early and then curtailed his activities to stay below the national spending limit. Hart kept his spending up longer than Mondale but ran into fund-raising difficulties. He borrowed almost $5 million in March, expecting a financial bonanza after his showing in the early primaries and caucuses. His fund raising did improve but not quickly enough to pay off the debt. Limited after March to spending what he could raise,

TABLE 4

DEMOCRATIC SPENDING AS PERCENTAGE OF STATE SPENDING LIMITS, 1984

Date	Mondale	Hart	Jackson
Primary states			
Feb. 28 (New Hampshire)	100	99	26
Mar. 13 (Ala., Fla., Ga., Mass., R.I.)	28	28	7
Mar. 20–Apr. 10 (Ill., Conn., N.Y., Pa.)	11	27	7
After Apr. 10 (12 states + D.C.)	6	15	7
Caucus states			
Feb. 20 (Iowa)	97	65	1
Mar. 4 (Maine)	95	27	0
After Mar. 4 (26 states)	7	10	2

NOTE: The information in this table may not be strictly comparable from candidate to candidate, because candidates use different methods of accounting. Jesse Jackson allocated only 19 percent of his spending against the state limits, Mondale 37 percent, and Hart 90 percent. Nevertheless, if we assume some internal consistency within each campaign, the table does give a sense of change over time for each.
SOURCES: Calculated from each candidate's Federal Election Commission reports of spending allocated against the various state spending limits, 1984 year-end reports filed in January 1985 for Jackson and Hart and the post–general election report filed in December 1984 for Mondale.

Hart's outlays dipped sharply after Pennsylvania's April 10 primary. Jackson raised and spent money at a steady rate of about $1 million per month for March through June.

What difference does it make if candidates spend heavily early but not during May and June? (In 1984 some large states with later primaries and caucuses included Texas, Colorado, Indiana, Maryland, Ohio, North Carolina, Nebraska, Oregon, West Virginia, New Jersey, and California.) One problem is that candidates seem to be spending their money before the public starts paying attention to the race. Except for the traveling press corps and other political junkies, most people choose not to spend their time early in an election year learning how primary candidates differ on the issues. By the time the campaign reaches most people, the voters know little about the candidates, and the candidates cannot afford to inform the voters.

These findings about spending patterns in the primaries directly parallel those Warren Miller reported earlier in this volume about what voters learned about the 1984 presidential candidates and when they learned it. Miller found that the voters learned little about the candidates before the general election campaign and most of what they did learn by Super Tuesday (March 13). No one has systematically studied the relation between spending and voters' information in presidential primaries, but the connections between Miller's findings and mine seem too close to be coincidental.

Either spending and contribution limits harm the amount of information voters acquire by keeping spending too low, or spending levels are irrelevant. Either way, the policy questions seem obvious: What good do the limits do? Are they enforceable? What are the costs of maintaining them? How do the costs and benefits balance? I turn first to the matter of enforcement.

Ways around the Limits

The campaign finance system leaves most candidates feeling short of money after the first round of primaries, if not before. One result has been to stimulate activities that fall outside the legal definition of contributions and expenditures. This decreases the effect of disclosure, decreases public accountability, and is ultimately bound to increase voters' cynicism.

Past elections have shown how spending and contribution limits increase a candidate's dependence on interest groups—particularly if a group can deliver volunteers, spend money communicating with its own members, or work with candidates on "nonpartisan" drives to increase registration and voter turnout in targeted districts.[3] Anything done along these lines in the past increased in 1984.

Most interest group activity outside the limits also escapes disclosure. It is impossible, for example, to put a dollar value on labor's efforts on Walter Mondale's behalf. I estimated labor's efforts for the Carter-Mondale ticket as being worth about $11 million in 1976, a number subsequently confirmed as approximately accurate in court depositions. Herbert Alexander put the value of the 1980 effort at about $15 million.[4]

Labor may well have spent as much during the 1984 primaries as it did during the whole 1976 or 1980 election, but the public will probably never know for sure. One possible indication is from the disclosed tip of the iceberg. Labor's reported communication costs on behalf of the Carter-Mondale ticket came to $1.1 million in 1976 and $1.5 million in 1980. Federal Election Commission (FEC) reports put the 1984 figure at $4.3 million. The AFL-CIO's national Committee on Political Education (COPE) reported spending $315,982 on communicating with members on Carter's behalf for all of 1976 and $382,120 for 1980. In 1984 COPE reported spending $475,634 for Mondale during March alone.

But 1984 was not just a continuation of the past. As in every election under the law so far, creative accountants and lawyers managed to dream up new ways to test the limits of limits. The best known were the 137 Mondale delegate committees that reported raising and spending about $700,000. The delegate committees registered themselves as "independent expenditure" committees, a designation that relieved them of having to abide by the contribution and spending limits for candidates. But after the press published reports of overlapping Mondale and delegate committee staff and Gary Hart filed a formal complaint with the FEC, the commission launched an investigation of the facts relating to each delegate committee's independence.

Mondale asked the committees to disband in April after he had suffered negative press on the issue for more than a month. The candidate and the commission continued to contest the legal issue for months, however, until they finally signed a consent decree in November, after the general election. Under the decree Mondale agreed to pay a civil fine of $18,500 and to return $379,640 in public financing to the Treasury. But the consent agreement—like most consent agreements—resolved none of the important legal issues. Mondale admitted nothing, the commission officially found nothing, and no legal precedents were set for the future. No future candidate would be likely to use delegate committees to get around the law's spending and contribution limits after the political price Mondale paid in 1984. But politicians did learn from this, as they have from other commission investigations, that future candidates can take less spectacular steps to test the law's boundaries without worrying about getting caught by the FEC before election day. This can only encourage legal technicians to look for new loopholes the next time around.

The year 1984 saw other new techniques introduced and old ones refined. There may be fewer big contributors in presidential politics, but there seem to be many more fund-raising entrepreneurs. According to one press report, Nathan Landow, a Maryland real estate developer, raised more than $1.5 million for Mondale's campaign, Duane Garret, a fine-art dealer, and Thomas Rosenberg, a Chicago real estate developer, raised $700,000 each, and so forth and so on.[5] The difference between a fund-raising entrepreneur and a large contributor has nothing to do with fat cats. In one case a wealthy person gives his or her own money; in the other a wealthy person taps wealthy friends for contributions knowing they will tap him for their own favorite causes in the future. The difference is that a contributor's role is disclosed but a fund raiser's is not.

Then there are candidate loans. I mentioned earlier that Gary Hart was able to raise almost $5 million on the expectation of future fund raising. John Glenn similarly received more than $2 million from three Ohio banks secured by his future expectations. In December 1984 Hart remained more than $4 million in debt and Glenn almost $3 million. The law says that a corporation may extend a candidate credit only in the ordinary course of doing business. But what is "ordinary" is judged by a corporation's normal practices with other clients. If a bank is willing to let businesses borrow on their expectations, this may become a difficult area for the FEC to monitor.

Monitoring a bank may be easier than monitoring someone who is dedicated to getting around the law. When political consultant Victor Kamber stopped working for Senator Alan Cranston's campaign late in 1983, Cranston owed the Kamber Group $114,443 and Custom Print, a Kamber affiliate, another $217,853. Kamber sued Cranston for payment. The candidate was obviously a bad credit risk, but if he could not get somebody to do more direct mail for him, his campaign was as good as over. At this point Stewart Mott stepped in. Mott is the General Motors heir, a coplaintiff in *Buckley* v. *Valeo*, who has underwritten many causes and candidates since giving Eugene McCarthy $210,000 during the 1968 primaries. Mott has helped support antinuclear groups and was attracted to Cranston's commitment to a nuclear weapons freeze. So when Cranston could not get money elsewhere, Mott Enterprises, a direct-mail business, let Cranston run up new bills of $130,415. How is the FEC to judge normal practices if a business is set up only to help favored candidates and causes by an owner who is willing to take a loss as his ordinary way of doing business?

Independent Expenditures

The first method for getting around limits that crosses most people's minds, however, is the independent expenditure. Mott himself spent more than $100,000 in this way in 1980. The Supreme Court's recent decision declaring independent spending to be protected by the First Amendment even if done by PACs in a publicly funded presidential race has lifted the last legal cloud from the continuation and growth of PACs.[6] Nevertheless, I would be surprised if independent spending by organized groups increased a great deal during general election campaigns. Conservative groups were able to tell potential contributors in 1980 that the only way they could help Ronald Reagan financially was by giving to an independently spending PAC. By 1984, however, people were being told repeatedly by the president and by Mondale that the best way to help was to give to the national parties. The 1979 amendments to the law allowed national parties to engage in all but unlimited spending for limited but clearly useful purposes. It would be surprising if independent spending by PACs grew very much in general elections in the face of that kind of competition.

Primaries may be a different story. Party organizations play little role before the nomination, and the candidates are starved for help. Spending limits, it should be clear, do not really limit spending; they channel it. In the general election the party channel is the easiest one for money to take. In primaries interest groups provide about the only ones available.

Although independent expenditures during primaries may grow, there is no way to begin estimating how much, or what the expenditures might mean politically. One reason is that we know so little about independent spending today. The FEC reports approximately $21.8 million in independent expenditures in 1984, $15.3 million of which was spent by PACs to support President Reagan and another $621,000 to oppose Walter Mondale. Of that $15.9 million in pro-Reagan or anti-Mondale spending, $13.7 million, or 86 percent, came from three groups: the National Conservative Political Action Committee

(NCPAC), the Fund for a Conservative Majority (FCM), and RuffPAC, a group founded in 1980 by Howard J. Ruff, a financial adviser.

These figures have often been cited in the press as if reported dollar figures are good indicators of political effort or effect. But there is no standard method of financial accounting for political campaigns or committees. As a result, the figures reported to the FEC can be highly misleading. We have already mentioned that organized labor seems to have spent about ten times as much on the past three presidential elections as it has been required to report. The disparities between reported and real spending are not as large for other interest groups, but they are nonetheless real. Corporate, trade association, and other PACs connected to ''parent'' organizations can pay their PACs' often substantial overhead costs with unreported funds from the parent organizations' treasuries. The groups' reported spending must be considered, therefore, to be somewhat of an understatement, although not as much as labor's.

Expenditures reported by unaffiliated ideological or issue groups probably *over*state their effect, particularly when they include fund-raising costs other groups are not even required to report. This can be seen by considering how NCPAC, RuffPAC, and FCM actually disbursed the money they reported as 1984 independent expenditures for Reagan or against Mondale. It should be emphasized that the funds included in table 5 include only activities the groups reported as independent expenditures, and not what they reported elsewhere on the FEC reports as organizational overhead.

When the press says that a group's independent expenditures total millions of dollars, many people seem to assume that the group spends money on roughly the same kinds of activities as does a candidate—television, radio and print media advertising, polling, consulting, and so forth. Candidates typically spend more than half their budgets on these activities. For the three conservative groups, the comparable figure was less than 10 percent.

The Fund for a Conservative Majority spent another 71 percent of its reported independent expenditures on telephones and phone banks. According to Robert Heckman, FCM's chairman, about one-fourth of the telephone money was spent for direct fund-raising appeals. The remaining $850,000 or so was spent for telephone calls to ask people if they wanted Reagan bumper stickers or, later in the year, to ask if they would be willing to canvass their neighborhoods to identify Reagan supporters.

In contrast with FCM, NCPAC and RuffPAC spent most of their money on direct mail. It is difficult for an outside observer to judge the political effect of direct mail with confidence. One is tempted to dismiss it as an effort in which the two PACs used President Reagan's name for their own fund raising and organization building. Neal B. Blair, the president of RuffPAC, told the *National Journal* that ''the primary purpose of the direct-mail effort was to raise funds; that was 60 per cent of it, and 40 per cent of it was to

TABLE 5

HOW INDEPENDENT EXPENDITURES FOR RONALD REAGAN OR AGAINST
WALTER MONDALE WERE SPENT BY THE THREE LARGEST INDEPENDENT
EXPENDITURE PACs, 1984

	National Conservative Political Action Committee	RuffPAC	Fund for a Conservative Majority
Reported 1984 spending for Reagan or against Mondale ($ millions)	10.1	2.1	1.6
Percentage distribution			
Mail services and printing	85	93	19
Telephone (including phone banks)	1	0	71
Payroll, office, travel	6	0	1
Other (including advertising other than by mail, consulting, miscellaneous)	8	7	10
Total	100	100	100

NOTE: Percentages may not add to 100 because of rounding.
SOURCE: Compiled by the author from Federal Election Committee reports.

get out the [pro-Reagan] bumper stickers and posters" that were included in
the appeals. NCPAC's finance director, L. Brent Bozell III, was quoted in
the same article as saying that "our goal was to use Ronald Reagan . . . as
the means of putting [back] together the conservative coalition" of the 1980
election.[7] NCPAC's chairman, John T. (Terry) Dolan, however, vehemently
resists these characterizations of his organization's mailings. Dolan said in
an interview with this author that he has no apologies for including a fund-
raising appeal with every letter he sends out but insisted that he uses mail
because he believes it to be politically the most effective way to spend his
money.

    Well over half of NCPAC's reported independent spending for Reagan
in 1984 went to the Richard A. Viguerie Company, to companies that get
contracts from Viguerie, or to the U.S. Postal Service. Like RuffPAC, which
also relied on Viguerie for its mail, NCPAC ended the year with a substantial
debt. (NCPAC's year-end debt was $4.2 million.) The largest number of
NCPAC mailings sent out by Viguerie were bulky, impressive-looking products wrapped in large manila folders. These contained a defense of Reagan's
record, bumper stickers, statements designed to make readers worry about
Democratic voter-registration efforts, an appeal for Reagan supporters to
register, a postcard addressed to state voter-registration officials asking for
information about how to register, a survey, and a fund-raising appeal. People

at NCPAC refer to the mailing as the "voter-registration package." Asked if he thought the mailing was the most efficient way to register people, fund-raising questions aside, Dolan said that he did. As evidence, he said that 3 percent of the people who sent their surveys back to the organization said (a) that they had not yet registered and (b) that the mailing had made them more likely to do so. Based on the thirty-eight cents NCPAC says each piece cost to mail and an assumed 3 percent rate for nonrespondents as well as respondents, that means NCPAC was spending $380,000 for every million pieces of mail to reach 30,000 unregistered potential voters. Of the 30,000, NCPAC estimates that 9,000 actually registered, a success rate that would be re-markably high, if true. (To be precise, a NCPAC press release estimated 250,000 new registrants for 28 million pieces of mail.) Accepting NCPAC's estimate of 9,000 registrants for each $380,000 spent as a working hypothesis, one might still question the efficiency *if registration were the only goal.* As a comparison, the national Republican party was able to reregister 54,179 converted Democratic voters and receive pledges from another 43,860 for about $750,000 in an effort some press reports labeled an "embarrassment."[8] Of course, NCPAC's program might have registered people and paid for itself at the same time, if the mailings had been successful. In addition, registration clearly was only one of several political goals served by the NCPAC mailing. More important, Dolan maintains that only he and the people who give money to his organization have any right to say how their money should be spent.

I agree with Dolan on this last matter but would add two caveats. First, my main point is not about legality or honesty or who has the right to question whom. Rather, it is to make readers aware that not all spending dollars are created equal. Second, on the question of honesty itself: even if no one intentionally deceived anybody else, I wonder whether the people who received NCPAC's and RuffPAC's letters knew that ninety cents of every dollar they might contribute was apt to be used for exactly the same kind of mailing they had just received. Or, as RuffPAC's president Blair said in a statement that goes beyond mine in questioning the sender's honesty as well as the recipient's knowledge: "It is dishonest to mail to people to say, 'This is an effort to fund X, Y, or Z' when your records show you are not going to be able to fund X, Y, or Z and when all you are doing is funding further mailing to try to reduce the debt. . . . They [groups in debt] are caught in this servitude where they have to continue to mail to service debt. They can reduce it some; but they don't feel good about little old ladies sending in their $10 bills when maybe $8 of that is going to go for more mailings."[9]

So the three largest conservative PACs may have reported a great deal of independent spending in 1984, but it is impossible to say much about the spending's political effect from the dollar amounts alone. This suggests that the importance of future spending may depend on which groups engage in exactly what efforts. But whatever the political effect, the nominal dollar value of these and other activities outside the law's contribution and spending limits seems likely to increase as the limits become progressively more constraining to candidates.

Recommendations

I have been talking in the past two sections about some indirect effects of contribution and spending limits. It seems difficult to justify the limits as a matter of policy if one of their main effects is to encourage voters—who think this is the only way they can help their favored candidate—to contribute by mail to a PAC that just turns around and spends the contributions on more postage. It seems equally hard to justify contribution limits that not only fail to eliminate "fat cats" but encourage them to engage in activities left unreported in FEC records. Finally, it seems difficult to defend contribution and spending limits set so woefully low that they encourage a dependency on interest group activities that defeat the purpose of disclosure.

These conditions make a very strong case for simply doing away with spending limits and with contribution limits for individuals (not PACs) during the presidential primary season. (I would not make this argument for the general election, when limits encourage giving to the parties.) Some worthy arguments support limits of some kind, however. Without limits front-runners and incumbents might gain too much of an advantage during the primaries. Once the nomination is assured, prospective nominees might use June and July to circumvent the limits that would remain for the general election. So perhaps it is premature to suggest a return to unregulated contributions and spending.

That is enough said about indirect effects; let us refocus our attention on what ought to come first. If there must be campaign finance limits, they should fit the delegate selection system. This point must be emphasized: campaign finance regulations should not be designed in a vacuum. They ought to be written with the aim of providing adequate funds for specific electoral circumstances. Conversely, party rules makers should consider the effects of campaign finance regulation when they tinker with delegate selection. Unfortunately, the two activities have been conducted so far in almost complete isolation from each other.

The present delegate selection system poses a more difficult logistical challenge to candidates than the general election. The irrelevance of the party label also makes the voters' job more difficult. It seems clear to me, therefore, that candidates would have to spend more money in the primaries than in the general election to inform voters equally well—not less money, as the law now provides.

How much more? One approach might be for Congress to do away with the national spending limit and leave the separate state limits in effect. State limits, though circumvented on the edges, seem important for giving dark-horse candidates a chance in the early contests. Keeping the state limits without a separate national limit would have tripled the 1984 national spending limit to about $60 million. It is worth mentioning that this is less than half the $131 million that winning Senate candidates spent through November in their most recent elections. Senate and presidential races are not really comparable, of course. But we are talking about two races covering the same constituencies, both of which get good press coverage. Senate winners are much better known to the voters than presidential primary candidates. Money must be at least one reason why.

Of course, raising the spending limit will not help candidates who have not yet reached the limit. The overall spending limit pinched Ford in 1976, Reagan in 1976 and 1980, and Mondale in 1984. For other candidates the more basic need has been for more money after the first round of primaries. One modest approach would be to double the federal match to a two-to-one ratio for money contributed between March 1 and June 1. The current public funding formula does not use up the money set aside for this purpose in the Treasury. If the checkoff is retained, excess Treasury money could be put to much better use this way in the future than by giving public funds to congressional candidates.

Both raising the spending ceiling and increasing the flow of money to candidates in the spring seem appropriate to the delegate selection task the parties now ask the candidates to undertake, but maybe the task itself needs to be addressed. If it would take $60 million to run an adequate campaign under the present system, do we really want a delegate selection system that would require candidates to engage in that level of fund raising before the nomination? Should people think instead about changing the system in a way that would help the public focus its attention and simplify the candidates' problems of communication without ruling dark horses out entirely?

From where I stand, these considerations lead me to think favorably (provided front loading can be reversed) about Representative Morris K. Udall's proposal to require all states that want primaries to hold them on the first Tuesday of March, April, May, or June. Concentrating the primaries should concentrate the public's attention and widen the audience for national debate broadcasts without placing the insurmountable hurdles in the path of a dark horse that a national primary would. Udall's proposal could go a long way, therefore, toward reducing the severe problems the national spending limit gave candidates in 1980 and 1984.

Whatever the specific decision, the present system needs change. Either the selection process should be simplified, or the finance limits should be markedly increased. The present mixture stimulates unaccountable behavior and destroys the purpose of disclosure. Most important, it fails to provide candidates with the resources they need to inform the public. We could debate whether the public should choose the party nominees. Under the post-1968 nominating system, the public is supposed to make the choice but has little basis for doing so. There is a complete mismatch between means and ends. This surely need not be so.

Notes

1. The exceptions were Jimmy Carter (1976), Ronald Reagan (1984), and Jesse Jackson (1984). Reagan in 1984 was unchallenged in the primaries and spent money late to help his general election campaign. Jimmy Carter in 1976 was a challenger who started out as a dark horse unable to raise early money. He also, therefore, was able to spend money late to help in the general election. Carter spent more than one-fourth of his 1976 total after June 30, when his nomination was assured and funds were easy to raise. Jackson was the only candidate in the table, therefore, who did not spend a disproportionately large percentage of his prenomination money early, largely because he did not have it to spend.

2. The campaign law contains separate spending limits for each state as well as an overall limit for the country. The state limits amount to a 1976 base of sixteen cents per person of voting age. Each year the sixteen-cent base is corrected for inflation (it was thirty-two cents in 1984), as is the national limit. In 1976 the national limit was about double the sum of the state limits. By 1984 the national limit was only one-third of the combined state limits because the state figures increase with population as well as inflation but the national limit grows only with inflation.

Gary R. Orren has also examined how spending changed over time during 1984 as a percentage of the state limits in "The Nomination Process: Vicissitudes of Candidate Selection," in Michael Nelson, ed., *The Elections of 1984* (Washington, D.C.: CQ Press, 1985), p. 45. For technical reasons, I present the data differently from Orren.

3. For a description of such interest group activity during the 1980 presidential primaries, see my "Looking Back at the Future of Campaign Finance Reform," in Michael Malbin, ed., *Money and Politics in the United States* (Chatham, N.J.: AEI/ Chatham House, 1984), pp. 253–55.

4. Michael J. Malbin, "Labor, Business, and Money—A Post-Election Analysis," *National Journal*, March 17, 1977, pp. 412–17; depositions taken in Republican *National Committee* v. *Federal Election Commission*, 487 F.Supp. 280 (S.D.N.Y. 1978) (see also Malbin, "Looking Back," p. 273, n. 57, for discussion); and Herbert E. Alexander, *Financing the 1980 Election* (Lexington, Mass: D.C. Heath, 1983), p. 338.

5. Peter Bernstein, "Fritz's Fat Cats Shake the Money Tree," *Fortune*, August 20, 1984, p. 153.

6. *Federal Election Commission* v. *National Conservative Political Action Committee, et al.* 470 U.S. _____, 105 S. Ct. 1459 (1985).

7. Ronald Brownstein, "On Paper, Conservative PACs Were Tigers in 1984—but Look Again," *National Journal*, June 29, 1985, p. 1506.

8. Bill Peterson, "GOP 'Open Door' Deemed Success Despite Shortfall," *Washington Post*, August 23, 1985, p. A3.

9. Brownstein, "On Paper," p. 1508.

Effects of the Present System of Campaign Financing on Special Interest Groups

Xandra Kayden

Historically, political reform has been directed at curbing powerful interests, and our most recent efforts are no exception to the rule. The major features of the Federal Election Campaign Act, as initially enacted, and as amended by Congress and by the federal courts in the 1970s, provide for limitations on contributions to campaigns and public disclosure of who is giving to whom in what amounts.

The law succeeded in curbing some interests, particularly in the presidential campaigns, as was intended, but it gave greater weight to others. It created a new avenue for participation—independent spending—which has been used by the newer groups predominantly, but which appears to be spreading to other groups and to other campaigns beyond that for the presidency.

The law gave visibility to the activity of interest groups through its disclosure provisions. This visibility has led some to believe the candidates are being taken over by the interests and others to believe the groups are a greater threat to the parties. This writer believes neither assertion is correct, but it is clear that campaign finance reform has altered the balance of power among the participants in the electoral process and raises serious questions about the nature of representative democracy. The biggest winners under the new rules are the two major political parties, and that may be the best news of all.

When we consider "the interests," we think of the balance of economic interests—particularly for business and labor—and of interests representing special concerns based on ethnicity, religion, social values, special status in the society (race, sex, age, disability), and so on. The effect of the campaign finance law, as seen in the 1984 election, has been to pit labor against the social groups of the right in presidential campaigns (with the social groups of the left playing a smaller role), and to shift the major activity of other interests to congressional and to state office races. Business interests contribute more to the presidential campaign than any other group making contributions (as opposed to spending money independently of the campaign), but all political action committee (PAC) money is insignificant in the overall picture of presidential fund raising. PAC spending on congressional races, however, rose 25 percent from the last congressional election in 1982, almost two-thirds of which went to incumbents to the overall benefit of the Democratic party.[1]

The interests seeking to get their message heard—as opposed to seeking to affect directly the outcome of legislation—tend to use independent spending in the presidential election as a vehicle. They have yet to influence significantly the outcome of an election (though we have yet to have a close election since independent spending became a factor), but they do influence its tone. Because of the visibility of the presidential race, what happens during the campaign becomes a model for every other campaign for the next four years. The techniques the campaign professionals develop, the themes they employ, the participants in the campaigns and the political parties, and frequently our attitudes as voters and citizens, are all derived from the presidential experience. For that reason, we need to consider the function of the participants in the presidential campaign with care and understanding.

All of the changes that have come about in American politics since Watergate and the implementation of the campaign finance law cannot be attributed solely to the legislation. We have changed as a society, and our technology has profoundly altered the way we campaign. With that caveat in mind, let us consider what has happened to the traditional and to the nontraditional interests in the past few presidential elections.

The Traditional Interests: Business and Labor

Richard Nixon spent $61 million in his 1972 bid for reelection, $36 million more than he spent in 1968, and $40 million more than Gerald Ford spent in 1976, when he ran for reelection with public financing under the new law.[2] Most of Nixon's money was raised from big business, and it was the target for the finance reform. Under the new law, individuals were limited to $1,000 contributions and groups to $5,000 contributions. The public financing provisions of the law placed a value on small contributions ($250 and under) from individuals that could be matched during the prenomination phase of the election and prohibited donations of any kind to the campaigns of the candidates during the general election.

Business had been prohibited from making campaign contributions throughout the century, but the loopholes in the law (to say nothing of the neglect of the law) made the prohibition largely irrelevant. Still, we do not know how much was given, how much was sought, and what happened afterwards. We do know that the desire to curb business participation has been constant, and we know that today contributions from corporate political action committees are relatively small in presidential elections, though they far outweigh the contributions of other PACs (see table 1).

The data are based on contributions made during the primaries and do not include spending during the general election, which exceeded $100 million in congressional campaigns in 1984.[3] Labor unions placed a slightly higher emphasis on the presidential races than on the congressional ones during this period, but the 1984 election was unusual because of the early endorsement of Walter Mondale by the American Federation of Labor and Congress of Industrial Organizations (AFL-CIO).

In 1980, nonparty committee contributions in the presidential primaries were a little more than $1½ million ($300,000 more than the 1984 figure), of which $304,485 went to Democrats and $656,982 went to Republicans (including $177,530 to John Connally who chose not to accept public financing and thus was far more interested in the larger, but nonmatchable PAC contributions than were the other candidates).[4]

The decline in PAC contributions from 1980 to 1984 undoubtedly reflects the politics of each election. An incumbent Democratic president with a serious challenger in Senator Edward Kennedy and a relatively open race among the Republicans created a different political climate from that of an incumbent Republican president without opposition in his party and an open race in the Democratic party with a strong front-runner in Walter Mondale. These differences point to the problem of drawing conclusions about the effect of the law from the experience of one or even two elections: the politics of the day are undoubtedly *the* most important factor in any given election.

One issue to consider is the changing balance between business and labor, and what any shift in participation may portend for the political process. Each side fears the influence of the other. Labor was concerned with the almost unlimited potential for the growth of corporate PACs. Labor PACs grew from approximately 210 in 1975 to 394 by the end of 1984, while corporate PACs increased from 89 to 1,682 and trade association PACs from 318 to 698 in the same period.[5] Many now believe the rate of growth of corporate PACs has leveled off, but the intitial concern was well founded, particularly if one adds in the trade association PACs, whose interests are frequently (though not always) identical with those of corporations.

Though the PACs are unbalanced in number, the distribution of their contributions has so far been more even. At least 90 percent of AFL-CIO money goes to Democrats; corporate and trade association PACs lean toward Republicans, giving more even-handedly, usually to incumbents. Labor usually gives at or near the $5,000 maximum; business contributions are frequently less than $1,000. The net effect favors Democrats, who do better with PAC funds as a proportion of their contributions to campaigns and to the party.

The effect of the campaign finance law on presidential selection extends beyond the issue of money. Business certainly gave more in the presidential race, but labor benefited by being a membership organization and may have

TABLE 1
PAC Contributions to Candidates in Federal Primary Elections, 1984

Committee Type	Number of Contributions by PACs	Contributions ($ thousands)				
		Total	Presidential	Congressional[a]	Republican[a]	Democratic[a]
Corporation	1,322	21,526	600	20,926	11,833	9,691
Labor	235	12,714	239	12,475	850	11,859
Nonconnected[b]	392	6,805	156	6,649	2,831	3,965
Trade, membership and health	468	13,759	153	13,606	6,647	7,105
Cooperatives	43	1,252	30	1,222	461	791
Corporations without stock	81	911	29	882	290	621
Total	2,541	56,967	1,207	55,760	22,912	34,032

a. Identified contributions for all candidates, of each major party, for national office.
b. Not affiliated with corporations, labor, or other associations.
Source: Federal Election Commission, "FEC Releases 18-Month PAC Study," press release, October 26, 1984, based on reports filed as of June 30, 1984.

had a greater influence than any other interest through its ability to turn out volunteers for voter registration, get-out-the-vote drives, and general campaign work. Both corporations and labor unions are permitted to spend unlimited amounts on internal communications to their employees and members advocating the election or defeat of candidates. According to Herbert Alexander, labor spent $1.3 million in 1980 on internal communications for the Carter campaign, out of $15 million spent altogether. Pro-Republican unions such as the Teamsters matched this outlay by spending $1.5 million in communications supporting the Reagan campaign. As far as we know, business spending did not come close.[6]

In 1984, $4.4 million was spent in internal communications for Mondale, against $170,000 spent for Reagan (see table 2).[7] This, plus the unreported labor spending, which probably exceeded the $15 million estimated in 1980, balanced better against the $15.7 million spent for Reagan largely by the New Right as independent expenditures; than it did against business expenditures.

Labor's fear of the influence of business in presidential elections, which has in the past led it to advocate changes in the law that often create new problems, has been overestimated since the implementation of the law. Big business is well aware of the danger it faces in appearing too powerful, and if corporate PACs can be said to hold one priority in common, it is their intent to stay out of trouble. There are, after all, other avenues of influence, and we have become sensitive since Watergate to those who would play with the

TABLE 2
TOTAL RECEIPTS OF CANDIDATES AND OTHER SPENDERS, 1984
(in thousands of dollars)

Candidate	Campaign Committees[a]	PAC[b]	Internal Communications	Independent Expenditures	National Party
Askew	3,200	1			
Cranston	8,000	300			
Glenn	14,100	300			
Hart	23,200	5	$(0.7)^c$	(41)	
Hollings	2,800	200			
Jackson	10,400	30	2		
McGovern	3,000	13		(0.9)	
Mondale	81,600[d]	122	4,400 (600)	800 (500)	2,800
Reagan	74,100[d]	528	170 (45)	15,700 (400)	6,900

a. Campaign committees includes the principal committee and the authorized committees.
b. The PAC figures are included in campaign income and are not additional funds.
c. Figures in parentheses are spending against the candidate.
d. The Mondale and Reagan figures include the $40.4 million each received in public financing for the general election.
SOURCE: From data supplied by the Federal Election Commission, April 5, 1985.

electoral process.

The AFL-CIO, under the leadership of Lane Kirkland, has taken a more aggressive political role than it did under George Meany, who believed its strength lay more in collective bargaining than in political action. Added to the interests of its leadership, labor has certain advantages in the current presidential selection process, principally its ability to turn out volunteers in primary and caucus contests. The timing and number of these events make it a herculean task for a campaign organization to undertake on its own, and few interests in the country can claim the experience and organizational ability of labor unions in helping campaigns. The National Education Association and United Auto Workers have been among the most active and successful unions in this regard, and the Teamsters have made significant contributions of such aid to the Republicans in recent years.

Labor's strength is business's weakness in the presidential selection system. Business cannot usually motivate its employees to participate in campaigns, and though corporate PACs give more and far outnumber the unions, the influence of specific corporations has been diminished by the law. The fact of the creation of corporate political action committees suggests that their influence will grow (assuming a united focus of that interest), if not in presidential campaigns, then in others.

Corporate PAC contributions have increased in size through the years as the PAC fund-raisers have grown more sophisticated in their appeals and as employees grow more accustomed to "giving at the office." Corporate PAC contributions have become more focused, as PAC decision makers have begun to learn how to make their contributions most effective. Although principally motivated by the desire to ensure legislative access and influence, these committees have also begun to work together in networks (helped along by their trade associations and both major parties) to support candidates likely to support them.[8]

Most scholars of corporate PAC behavior point out the relative lack of political sophistication of their managers;[9] but that will probably change. As early as 1978, it was clear that many corporate PACs were reserving their funds until the end of the election period, which surprised both the campaign managers and the Republican party; the party had advocated they reserve a quarter of their funds for "risk" candidates, that is, challengers who might look more competitive toward the end of the election than they did in the beginning.[10] As corporate PACs grow in experience, they will probably become increasingly successful in fund raising and more interested in spending their money in ways likely to increase their influence. Given the constraints in presidential campaigns, corporate PACs are likely to become more active in congressional and, particularly, in state legislative races where their effect is bound to be greatest because of the low visibility such races have. The $5,000 a PAC can give to a presidential campaign weighs very little in the context of a national election. Many states do not have limits, but even in those that do, corporate PAC money would be more important because it comes into a much smaller pool.

The Nontraditional Interests

The variety of interests participating in American politics extends well beyond business and labor on the one hand and the groups of the New Right on the other, yet these two sets of groups trouble us the most. If we were to survey the variety of interests participating in electoral politics, we would recognize groups devoted to single issues, such as the environment and world peace, and to an increased role in the political process for their members, and so on. What draws our attention to the groups of the New Right is not their concerns, but the way they participate.

What distinguishes traditional from nontraditional in this context is not what the group cares about, but what it does. The behavior of the newer groups has been shaped in large part by the changes in the political environment: the new technology and the campaign finance law. That these groups frequently—perhaps invariably—express controversial views is a consequence of their cause for being: if more established groups had represented their views (groups such as the parties or other older organizations), they would have no raison d'être. That these groups use tools different from those of the more established groups for attaining their objectives is a reflection of the times in which they came into being and of the values, attitudes, and practices of the times in which the older groups came into being. The older groups established their standard operating procedures in the context of another struggle and another set of rules. Some have adapted to the newer way of doing things. AMPAC, for example, the American Medical Association's political action committee, is one of the oldest PACs in the country—second only to the AFL-CIO's Committee on Political Education (COPE)—and has been a leader in using independent spending. Most of the traditional groups, however, have followed the old ways of making contributions to candidates and of appealing to their members for support.

It has yet to be shown definitively that the newer ways are more effective in changing the outcomes of elections or influencing the behavior of elected officials; but there is no question they are effective in raising money, and they spend a great deal of it, often independently of the campaigns and the parties. They are having some effect in expressing their views and in determining the nature of political debate.

Our concern is with who they are, what they are doing, and whether or not it alters the balance of interests we believe underlies the stability of our system of government. Our assumption is that they are a product of our political times and that the campaign finance law has not only molded their behavior, but added to their strength relative to others. If there is an imbalance, the law is partly to blame.

Who They Are. Most of the groups we would label nontraditional call themselves members of the New Right: the National Conservative Political Action Committee (NCPAC), the Fund for a Conservative Majority, the Moral Majority, and so on. Some, such as the Moral Majority, are membership organizations; most are not. They are based in Washington and consist of a small staff of professionals with access to a very large mailing list. They may have boards of directors, but the boards rarely meet.

A number of these groups were formed in the mid-1970s, in the aftermath of Watergate, when some of the surviving professionals in the Republican party feared the decline in their ranks and the power of organized labor. They wanted to balance that power by raising and spending more money.[11] Some of the motivation for the emergence of these groups was a reaction to the perceived shift to the left in policy and in social attitudes of the 1960s and early 1970s. The expected realignment and reemergence of a dominant Republican party had not occurred, and they felt it needed help.

Whatever the relationship between these groups and the GOP in the early days, by the late 1970s some in the party, particularly party chairman William Brock, began to feel they also constituted a danger to the party. Richard Viguerie, the direct mail leader who made possible much of the New Right's success in fund raising, talked about working around the party if it did not conform. Concern was expressed that the direct mail solicitations "miseducated" and raised expectations that could not be met.[12]

What They Do. All of the nontraditional groups are not on the New Right, but most are by far. Whether or not their relationships are strained with the GOP, they support it almost as uniformly as the AFL-CIO supports Democrats. They spend far more than any other single participant and are responsible for most of the independent spending. In the 1980 and 1984 elections, the top five independent spenders were New Right groups, ranging from NCPAC, which spent $9.7 million in 1984, to the Christian Voice Moral Government Fund, which spent $340,000, mostly to influence the outcome of the presidential election.

"Independent expenditures," according to the law, are expenditures supporting the election or defeat of a candidate that are made independently of the candidate or his or her committee. They were not part of the legislation originally enacted, but grew out of the Supreme Court ruling in *Buckley* v. *Valeo* in 1976, upheld in 1985 by a ruling in a case brought originally by the Federal Election Commission and the Democratic party against NCPAC and the Fund for a Conservative Majority.

Although some contend that the original intent of the Court was to preserve local political activity, independent spending has been the purview of the Washington-based groups almost exclusively. The basis of the Court's position is that the First Amendment right of free speech must be equated with the cost of communication in our society. Limiting the amount of money one can spend limits one's ability to communicate. Of the $18.5 million spent independently in 1984, $16.5 million was spent for the election or defeat of Ronald Reagan and Walter Mondale. Of that sum, $15 million was spent on Reagan's behalf.[13] In 1980, when the first extensive independent spending in the presidential election took place, 85 percent of the money spent on Reagan's behalf was spent during the general election. In 1984, however, only $6½ million, or 40 percent, was spent during the general election, which suggests a change in either the campaign or the fund-raising strategies of these groups.[14]

One of the arguments against independent spending—and the campaign finance law—is that the prohibition against contributions during the general election to a candidate who opts to rely on public financing has prompted the nontraditional groups to raise and to spend money independently of the campaign. The 1984 experience, however, seems to belie that argument. Sixty percent of the independent spending was done before the Republican convention in the third week of August, before the prohibition against making donations to the candidate came into effect. It may be true that the direct mail solicitations that finance groups of the New Right urge their respondents to contribute because independent spending is the only avenue open to them, but the prohibition does not govern the behavior of the groups in question.

Controversy about independent spending rests on three issues: (1) the nature of the appeal; (2) the consequences of spending large amounts of money outside the normal channels of campaign spending and the question of accountability it raises; and (3) the basic discomfort such spending evokes in campaign managers who have a difficult time controlling those within the campaign and view independent expenditures as potential "wild cards" in their campaign strategies.

Appeals. Most of the groups making independent expenditures raise their money through the mail, and most of their appeals are based on a negative charge. The motivation for giving large sums in politics was that it bought access. Since "small" money does not buy access, the motivation for giving it must be something else, and the tradition in American fund raising has been to appeal to one's sense of outrage. The small donor derives satisfaction—a moral uplift—from contributing to a campaign. The issues that provide satisfaction are apt to be issues in which the donor is in the minority. After all, if one is in the majority, why worry?

Direct mail solicitations are based, then, on minority appeals, which frequently mean controversial positions. They also have the capacity to galvanize a public that might be generally anti-establishment, but might not otherwise really care about the specific issue. There is the danger that such appeals are increasing the polarity in political debate; they are certainly not likely to promote consensus.

Accountability. Elections can be viewed as the public's expression of the credibility of one candidate over another. When all the shouting is over, the voter makes a choice, and the winner risks being held accountable in the next election for what he or she said in the last campaign. The most frequently quoted comment about independent spending was made by one of its most effective advocates, John T. (Terry) Dolan, director of NCPAC:

> Groups like ours are potentially very dangerous to the political process. We could be a menace, yes. Ten independent expenditure groups, for example, could amass this great amount of money and defeat the point of accountability in politics. We could say whatever we want about an opponent of a Senator Smith and the Senator would not have to say anything. A group like ours could lie through its teeth and the candidate it helps stays clean.[15]

Whether the independent spending groups did or do "lie through their teeth," there is no question that the fear exists that they will, and if they do,

95

the campaign period is too short for the offended candidate to make that clear. After the election it will not matter; a recall election based on the invalid assertions of an outside participant just is not part of our process.

The independent spenders are seeking to influence the debate in an election, and the Supreme Court has held that their right to do so is inviolable. A more subtle difficulty with their participation, however, is that such groups (or any group, for that matter) do not stand to be affected directly by the outcome of the election. They appear to be more neutral, and, given the nature of opinion formation, their apparent disinterest gives them greater weight. We know enough to balance the views of the candidates who are actually contesting the election; we are less equipped to balance the views of third parties.

An added problem is the relative freedom in spending that independent expenditures provide. PACs contributing to campaigns are limited to $5,000 per campaign. Presidential campaigns face expenditure limitations in the primaries and have an overall ceiling with the public financing in the general election. The $9.7 million spent by NCPAC in the 1984 election was not an insignificant sum relative to other groups, and relative to the campaigns. It could make a difference in a close election.

Although presidential campaigns attract the bulk of independent spending, such spending probably matters the least in these campaigns because of their visibility and the opportunity voters have to make up their minds based on a wide array of information. Potentially, independent spending is more effective in races with less visibility because the message it sends will have less interference from alternative views. It is not an irrelevant fact that independent spending in congressional races almost doubled from 1980 to 1984, from $2.3 million to $4.5 million, while rising only marginally in the presidential campaign, from $16 million to $18.5 million.[16] We have no way of knowing what is spent in state races where reporting is not a federal responsibility.

The last aspect of accountability is the consequence of a national organization raising money and spending it in a particular election district. It is a problem we have yet to come to terms with in all interest group giving, but it is particularly noticeable in independent spending because groups are often able to put large amounts of money into a campaign and visibly target particular candidates, such as liberal senators in recent elections.

The question addresses the nature of representative government. National interests have always been focused on the members of Congress whose committee assignments affect their activity, but the growth of PACs, the institutionalization of their activity, the limitation the law places on individual contributions, and the rising costs of campaigning have made us more aware of the potential conflicts in our expectation of representation. Whose responsibility is it to worry about the activity of a representative or a senator who serves on a banking committee? The district from which he or she comes may have interests that conflict with national priorities, or at least with the priorities of the more powerful interests affected by the committee.

It is a complex question to which some of the independent spenders respond by speaking of ''social'' as opposed to ''geographic'' precincts. According to this argument, geographic boundaries are outdated. Those sharing social interests may find themselves in the minority in any given election district, but if they unite, they can find a district where they can be in the majority. The danger is a tyranny of the minority, especially when the majority cannot hold the minority accountable through the electoral process.[17]

We lean to the obvious answer that the geographic district is the one upon which the Constitution is based, but the nature of our society is so complex that this answer may not be sufficient in the long run. At some point, we may want legislation that limits the proportion of outside participation in congressional elections. Doing it, however, will be a tricky business, given the First Amendment, the mobility of the interests, and the complexity of our political life.

Wild cards. Perhaps the least serious complaint about independent expenditures is the fear campaign managers have about them. Campaigns are temporary organizations that operate under varying degrees of sophistication in dealing with uncertainty. Polling data has become very important in decision making throughout a campaign. It is used to determine the effect of every public appeal. Outsiders, who by definition are not involved with the campaign, are not likely to be attuned to the specifics and frequently have their own message to get across anyway.

Trying to control the views of those inside a campaign is a herculean effort under the best of circumstances. Trying to cope with the activities of would-be friends outside only complicates the task. In 1984 some campaign managers called potential independent spenders to a meeting to explain their strategy and, consequently, to make clear to them that making an expenditure at that point would be illegal because of the meeting.

In all fairness, however, most of the groups that make independent expenditures routinely have moved carefully into the field. Some, such as AMPAC, have assumed traditional campaign activities (such as publishing a list of doctors supporting a candidate). Some focus more on their opposition to a candidate and ignore the opponent who will benefit from their participation. Some employ the same professionals who manufacture the ads used by campaign organizations, and their ads are frequently indistinguishable in form and substance from what one would expect from the campaign.

The fear campaign managers have of independent spending may decline with experience and with acceptance of the organizations that make them. It is unlikely those constrained by the law in giving and spending will ever be completely at ease with the unlimited spending of others; but familiarity breeds acceptance, particularly when there is very little that can be done about it as long as the courts uphold the right to spend and Congress fails to develop an alternative curb on "independent" behavior.

Has the Campaign Finance Law Altered the Balance of Power?

The purpose of the campaign reform law was to control the interests. What it has achieved is an ordering of the behavior of interests, and perhaps that is all we could reasonably expect. Elizabeth Drew has argued that the law has turned our elected officials into an uncontrollable herd, barreling down on the interests for money, distorting the nature of democracy.[18]

Others such as Michael Malbin of the American Enterprise Institute, have suggested that the law has only disclosed a pattern of behavior with which we have lived all along. It is likely that the law has been successful in curbing some of the excesses of some of the groups, particularly business, which may have been victimized by greedy politicians as frequently as it indulged its political interests. The point is that since we do not know with certainty what went on before, we cannot measure the change.

What we do know is that the institutionalization of political action committees has created a new industry in American politics. PAC fund-raisers, attorneys, and accountants have developed into a professional cadre of participants who know the rules of the game and apply them with increasing awareness as each election cycle passes. The professionalism itself may turn out to be the best hedge against excess, because the participants expect to be around from one election to the next and are less likely to view any given election as *The One* they have to win.

The only institution likely to be threatened by interest group behavior is the political party, and this writer believes quite firmly that the two major political parties are stronger than they have ever been nationally and are growing stronger at the state level.

The revitalization of the parties was due in large part to the law, which made the parties far more important in elections than the interests. No other organization can bring to an election the resources and skills available to the party. No other can spend as much on the candidates in coordination with the campaign (NCPAC and independent spending notwithstanding). No group has the integral, legal place of the parties in the nominating process, even for the presidency, the one nomination over which the parties have least control.

If the interests cannot dominate the parties, however much they may appear to in the negotiations surrounding our selection of presidential nominees (we need to distinguish between politicking to form a coalition for governance and the seeking of some kind of invisible, subversive influence), can they dominate the candidates? Alternatives are frequently suggested, such as increasing the limits on individual contributions, which would undoubtedly alleviate some of the problem. Public financing does not appear to be as critical to the exercise of independent spending as we thought, if the experience of the 1984 election proves to be the wave of the future and the spending occurs before prohibitions against contributions are imposed. If public financing were extended to Congress, PAC money would certainly decline in campaigns, but the search for influence would probably take some less visible avenue.

The best hope may lie in the openness of the disclosure provisions. If the voters have confidence that they know who is backing the candidates, they will be served as well as we can serve them, short of substantially altering the campaign finance system. Perhaps the next reform should be to extend disclosure to the states so that, for instance, contributions now made to state parties at the behest of the national campaign or of the national party that cross state lines are reported in a centralized and orderly manner.

If we have altered the balance among the interests—giving greater weight to membership organizations, such as labor, over nonmembership organizations, such as business—the sheer increase in business PACs has been a counterbalance. The independent spending groups were themselves designed to balance labor, and they may have succeeded in spending more, but even in elections there is a limit to how much money can buy. What the New Right and labor can provide in resources to their respective party choices aids the campaigns but leaves each group's issues somewhat out of balance. It is not what James Madison had in mind when he wrote the tenth *Federalist* paper, arguing that one side in an issue will be balanced against the other.

If there is a danger in the behavior of interests it is not in the presidential campaigns; it appears lower down on the ladder and increases as the visibility of the candidates declines. The law has created new organizations. The first object of any organization is to maintain itself, and if these new organizations find themselves less than satisfied with their influence in the presidential selection process, they will look to other fields. The greatest danger exists in state legislative campaigns where a little money goes a very long way, and where more and more of our policies may be decided if we continue the process of federal deregulation. Presidential elections set the tone of electoral debate and provide the experience for campaign professionals. In that regard, presidential elections are critical to the participation of interests, even if their muscle will be flexed elsewhere.

Notes

1. Margaret Lawton, Paul Risley, Lorri Staal, and Lisa Peterson, "PAC Contributions to 1984 House and Senate Candidates: January 1, 1983 through November 22, 1984" (Congress Watch Study, January 3, 1985, mimeographed).

2. Herbert E. Alexander, *Financing Politics: Money, Elections, and Political Reform*, 2d ed. (Washington, D.C.: CQ Press, 1980), p. 5.

3. Lawton et al., "PAC Contributions."

4. Federal Election Commission, "FEC Report: Final Report on the Presidential Pre-Nomination Campaign, 1979-80," October 1981, p. 4. Additional funds went to candidates not affiliated with either major party.

5. Federal Election Commission, "FEC Says PAC's Top 4,000 for 1984," January 28, 1985.

6. Herbert E. Alexander, "Making Sense about Dollars in the 1980 Presidential Campaign," in Michael J. Malbin, ed., *Money and Politics in the United States: Financing Elections in the 1980s* (Washington, D.C.: Chatham House/American Enterprise Institute, 1985), pp. 22–23.

7. Drawn from data supplied by the Federal Election Commission, April 5, 1985. The author is grateful for the prompt and professional assistance of Michel Dickerson of the Public Records Division of the FEC.

8. Frank J. Sorauf, "Accountability in Political Action Committees: Who's in Charge?" (Paper delivered at the Annual Meeting of the American Politial Science Association, 1982).

9. See, for example, Theodore J. Eismeier and Philip H. Pollock, III, "Political Action in Committees: Varieties of Organization and Strategy," in Malbin, *Money and Politics in the United States*, p. 123.

10. Xandra Kayden, "The Impact of the FECA on the Growth and Evolution of Political Action Committees," in *An Analysis of the Impact of the Federal Election Campaign Act, 1972-78* (Cambridge, Mass.: Institute of Politics, John F. Kennedy School of Government, Harvard University, 1979), prepared for U.S. Congress, House of Representatives, Committee on House Administration.

11. Xandra Kayden and Eddie Mahe, Jr., *The Party Goes On* (New York: Basic Books, 1985).

12. Xandra Kayden, "Campaign Finance: The Impact on Parties," in *An Analysis of the Impact of the Federal Election Campaign Act, 1972-78*, p. 98.

13. Data compiled from Federal Election Commission, "Independent Expenditure Index by Committee/Person Expending," March 4, 1985.

14. Ibid.

15. John T. Dolan, reported in the *Washington Post*, August 10, 1980, p. Fl.

16. "Independent Expenditure Index"; and Xandra Kayden, "Independent Spending," in *Financing Presidential Campaigns: An Examination of the Ongoing Effects of the Federal Election Campaign Laws Upon the Conduct of Presidential Campaigns* (Cambridge, Mass: Institute of Politics, John F. Kennedy School of Government, Harvard University, January 1982), prepared by the Campaign Finance Study Group for U.S. Congress, Senate, Committee on Rules and Administration.

17. Kayden, "Independent Spending."

18. Elizabeth Drew, *Politics and Money: The New Road to Corruption* (New York: Macmillan, 1984).

The Media and the Nominating Process

Michael W. Traugott

The importance of the news media in the current presidential nominating process has grown rapidly, to the point that many consider the media to be the major institutional force at work in selecting our national leader. The candidates still require the votes of participants in primaries and caucuses to secure delegates at their respective nominating conventions, but the major means of communicating with large numbers of potential voters is through the media.[1] Increasingly, communication strategies distinguish between particular messages for local electorates and broad themes for a national audience.

A Changing Campaign Environment

Any discussion of the contemporary role of the media in the presidential selection process has to account for the "new" nominating system in effect since the 1976 campaign. We have seen it in operation in the campaigns of only three electoral cycles, which presents a substantial problem for drawing generalizations from it. The essential elements of the new system are the changes in campaign financing due to the Federal Election Campaign Act (FECA) and its amendments, especially its spending limitations; the movement toward bound delegates, which began with the post-McGovern rules of the Democratic party and their implementation by the states in more numerous primaries and caucuses; and the declining influence of national party organizations in the nominating process, which resulted in part from the first two changes.

The combination of these forces has extended the campaign period, forced candidates to organize independent staffs and solicit funds sooner and on their own, and obligated them to travel more extensively than in the past. Because the limitations on spending affect the amount of advertising that can be purchased, the candidates have increased their reliance on the news media for early and frequent exposure to sustain their campaign efforts.

A Changing Media Environment

It is equally important to understand that the media environment in which these campaigns are taking place is also changing. Candidates' activities receive immediate national coverage, consisting of a common and homogeneous content presented through the reports of television network correspondents and wire service reporters. There are other, perhaps more subtle, shifts taking place as well, including an increase in the reporting of survey results on the relative standing of the candidates.

The combination of these forces has increased the importance of early decisions and actions by candidates. In addition to the organizational demands, there is pressure on the candidates to win early and often to establish and maintain name recognition and to develop momentum, or at least the perception of it. Strategically, candidates have to plan around the consequences of the front-loaded primary schedule, established more or less independently by the states. They also have to operate within the constraints of FECA expenditure limitations in the states. No wonder the "new" system has been described as demonstrating a clear bias toward unemployed or underemployed candidates for the highest office in the land.

The news media have become central actors in this process, both nationally and locally, because of the chronology of the primaries. They provide information about the candidates, about both their positions and their style, to a public that is relatively uninformed about many of them and relatively uninterested in the process of electing a president at this stage of the game. In the ebb and flow of the primary and caucus process, the national electorate learns who the candidates are and what they stand for through their ability to generate coverage and the reporting of their success in the early races. Residents of some states learn more about the candidates than residents of others because of idiosyncrasies in the schedule. The position of one's state on the primary and caucus calendar has something to do with what one knows and when one knows it.

The media also establish standards of performance for the candidates and report on their progress in meeting them. In this limited but important way, they have replaced the parties in the candidate selection process through their effects on winnowing the field.[2] This is not an unreasonable role for some political institutions to play, but the fundamental question is whether the criteria of newsworthiness, the pressures of meeting deadlines, and policies for allocating news space should be as important as they are in determining eventual success in the presidential nominating process.

The Relationship between the Media and the Candidates

The relationship between reporters and candidates has frequently been described as symbiotic. From the candidates' perspectives, the elements of the new system that include the lengthening of campaigns, the need for independent organizations and fund-raising operations, and the relationship between perceptions of viability and investment decisions by prospective volunteers and contributors all dictate the need to establish broad public recognition as early as possible. Under the previous system, familiarity with local leaders and organizations was an advantage, and the ascendancy of political unknowns was relatively rare. Outsiders and lesser-known candidates now can try to use the media to establish recognition and credibility through the generation of "free" coverage. This visibility is important to fund raising because perceptions of a candidate's likelihood of success affect decisions to contribute both time and money to a campaign.

These early investments are important for a number of reasons. An experienced staff is a precious commodity for any candidate, but the pool of potential staff members with presidential campaign experience is limited. Early commitments are a valuable resource for the candidate, and, of equal importance, an indicator to the media of initial judgments about the candidate by campaign professionals. Money is obviously important because of all the campaign necessities it buys. Not the least of these are travel, consultants, and controlled media—advertising—to build recognition and to structure and deliver the candidate's own targeted messages.

The media have an interest in their relationships with presidential candidates because electoral politics, and presidential contests in particular, make good news. That is to say, campaigns and elections lend themselves to coverage because the events and participants fulfill all of the basic criteria of newsworthiness.[3] The eventual outcome has a significant effect on Americans' lives. The process and the rules of the game are relatively straightforward and simple to understand and do not require extensive clarification for readers and viewers. The process operates on a predetermined schedule that permits rational organization of media resources to produce news. The contests involve conflict, but there tend to be relatively clear winners and losers, especially as vote counting and delegate accumulation proceed in the primaries and caucuses. The candidates are generally known and visible figures, the more so as the process moves along; and they and their staffs are almost always willing sources.

Candidates who understand the ways of the press and the institutional and personal needs of media professionals can increase the probability of receiving coverage by facilitating the job of reporters. Implementation of such a strategy frequently depends on the campaign's ability to organize and schedule activities to fit the deadlines of the press. This is increasingly done with an eye toward the production needs or demands of the evening news, and it frequently includes production of "pseudo-events"[4] or "medialities."[5] This means attempting to schedule major events no later than lunch or early afternoon, arranging for good crowds, and distributing prepared copies of the text, if there is one, in advance. For television, it means arranging a setting with appropriate visuals that will generate videotape with good pictures that can be used on the air.

Leubsdorf describes four phases in the relationship between politicians and the press in the nominating process.[6] For the purposes of this discussion, the first three phases are of greatest interest: the period (now lengthening) before the first primaries are held, the early primary period, and the late primary period leading up to the convention. Each of these phases has characteristic differences in the access reporters have to the candidates, in the relative interests of television versus print reporters, and in the quantity and quality of coverage that result. While the relationship between candidates and reporters is symbiotic, the mutuality of their interests is not uniformly distributed across the prenomination calendar.

In the first phase, which has already begun for 1988, most candidates lead a relatively lonely existence, traversing the country lining up staff members, supporters, and contributors. So far in advance of the "events" themselves (primaries and caucuses), the media do not have a substantial interest in generating large quantities of coverage. Most of what is written early reflects scorekeeping on who is "in" or thinking about getting in and who is "out" or withdrawing an early trial balloon. Most of the coverage will appear only in major national newspapers because they will be the only ones with sufficient resources to send a reporter into the field in the year before the primaries; other coverage can be found in the local press of the states the candidates are visiting. The coverage will generally be positive or no worse than neutral, if it does not include extended references to whether or not the candidate stands a serious chance of winning the nomination. Right from the start, candidates begin a two-track strategy of generating national visibility to sustain a public part of the campaign and of obtaining local coverage to gain supporters and build an organization in key states.

In the second phase, the television correspondents move in, as do many print reporters. The coverage now is organized by states in conjunction with the calendar of primaries and caucuses. The networks become crucial here, particularly with their special coverage of the Iowa caucuses and the New Hampshire primary. Access becomes more difficult for some journalists, and a distance develops between the candidates and the press. While the demand for content increases, a new set of rules for allocating coverage emerges. Expectations of performance dictate the distribution of coverage. Front-runners receive a larger proportion of story content and appear more often in the lead and in headlines than do those farther back in the pack. Viability becomes a crucial factor in the allocation of coverage, and then actual performance in these initial contests further dictates the structure and tone of this early reporting.[7]

As the primaries and caucuses actually get underway, a bifurcation in coverage styles is increasingly visible. The network broadcasts on the nights of the events present an immediate summary of results, both of the day's events and of the process since it began. The scheduling of interviews, the characterization of the success and status of the candidates by the correspondents, and the nature of the questioning are important elements in the winnowing process. For print reporters the benefit of a few more hours before deadline or the opportunity to write for a Sunday edition often leads to greater analysis, even if no less a preoccupation with the relative standing of the candidates.

In the third phase of the process, beginning around the first week in April and extending through the nominating conventions, reporting becomes more difficult and the coverage more critical. The candidates and reporters become more distant, not just because of the size of the traveling entourages but because of their changing roles. The chance of winning it all now makes the remaining candidates cautious and concerned about committing strategic errors, including misquotations and misstatements. Reporters are now dealing with potential presidents, and their criteria of evaluation of the candidates shift in subtle ways that lead to more critical coverage. There are also indications that the content of the news shifts from the earlier preoccupation with strategy and the elements of the "game" to somewhat greater emphasis on issues as the importance of the general election that lies ahead affects the coverage of current events.[8] Readers and viewers become more interested in the potential of the remaining candidates to serve, in response to the shifts in the coverage.

Reporting Styles and the Nature of Coverage

The relationship between reporters and candidates, the demands of news organizations, and the application of criteria of newsworthiness lead to the characteristic content of the reporting of campaigns and elections, which has been observed throughout the media and for different offices. The essential elements of much of this coverage are that it is event driven, is preoccupied with strategy and other dimensions of the game, is concentrated on the relative standings of the candidates, and is highly personalized rather than issue oriented.[9]

Arterton has devised a classification scheme for the reporting styles journalists use to describe the candidates' progress.[10] Understanding these conventions provides candidates with at least the possibility of affecting the content of the coverage they receive and therefore the perceptions of political and media elites about their viability. The basic elements of "horse race journalism" center on the media's use of "scenarios," "standards," and "benchmarks." These reportorial devices provide a convenient shorthand for communicating the relative standing of the candidates to readers and viewers.

105

Nowhere is this clearer than in the use of scenarios, which are the prospective strategic paths by which the candidates hope to secure the nomination. They construct these plans in order to convince journalists of their viability. In Arterton's terminology, these include strategies for such eventualities as an "outright win" based upon victories in the early primaries and caucuses, a "winnowing" process resulting from an extended battle in the primaries before the candidate can emerge victorious late in the process but before the convention, or the "brokered convention" scenario, based upon no clear winner emerging from the primaries. By and large, the front-runners expect a clear victory while those farther back in the pack expect to have to wait a little longer to reap the fruits of their labor through the attrition or errors of their opponents. It is the job of reporters to evaluate these scenarios, on their own merits and in relation to the strategic plans of the other candidates.

Standards are simple, easily understood measures of candidate success that can be communicated to readers or viewers. Before the primaries and caucuses begin, the most obvious standards are success in fund raising, the point at which the conditions are met for receiving matching federal funds, the size of organizations, and the quality of key campaign personnel. Assessments of acknowledged party leaders and activists, especially their endorsements, are also important. One set of standards that can be observed with increased frequency is results of preference questions in surveys conducted by the media as well as the results of surveys done for others, including the candidates.

Once balloting begins, standards become even easier to employ. These include the number of votes received and the number of delegates pledged. While the correspondence between these two measures is not complete because of the idiosyncrasies in the formulas for delegate allocation, which vary from state to state, together they provide an easy and convenient means of reporting who is ahead and by how much. They provide an important quantitative cue for further evaluation of scenarios, in conjunction with how much money each of the candidates has left and his current cash flow position.

The suitability, reliability, and relative accuracy of these indicators increase as the process moves along. As the field narrows, the choices become more obvious, and the comparative standings easier to discern. One clear consequence of these trends is that allocation of coverage more closely approximates candidate rankings on these indicators. The winners' names appear in the headlines and in the lead, and coverage is allocated proportionately according to the order of finish.

Scenarios and standards are combined continuously throughout the prenomination phase to formulate expectations of performance for each candidate. The actual turn of events can then be compared with these expectations, or benchmarks, to assess the candidates' more or less orderly progress toward the nomination. This is a form of agenda setting in which momentum is established and maintained as long as expectations are met or exceeded. Candidates understand the significance of the media in establishing these benchmarks as well as in communicating scenarios and standards. The symbiotic relationship between candidates and reporters is reflected, however, in the campaigns' interests in orchestrating coverage that sustains momentum.

Mass Media Content: The Quantity and Quality of Coverage

The content of the products of journalists and the media who cover the presidential nominating process have undergone extensive analysis during the new campaign period.[11] In all of these studies, a consistent set of findings enables us to generalize about the coverage candidates receive on network news and in major national papers, as well as in selected local media.

The most important characteristic about the content of this coverage is its preoccupation with the game elements of the campaign process itself, including strategy. Patterson reported that a majority of the 1976 coverage (between 51 and 59 percent of the news he looked at) was devoted to winners and losers, strategy and logistics, and campaign appearances and publicity. Only about one-fifth of the coverage was devoted to coverage of issues or policy. There were no significant differences between press and network coverage. Robinson made similar findings in his study of CBS and UPI coverage of the 1980 campaign. He also shows that coverage of issues has consistently received short shrift in the media since World War II.

This distribution of content results from criteria of newsworthiness and assessments of what interests the audience. One way of putting it, as Robinson does, is that "seriousness does not sell."[12] It is also true, however, that in the prenomination phase, the issue differences between candidates from the same party are relatively muted, compared to their differences with the positions of candidates from the other party. Furthermore, the candidates tend to deliver very similar policy pronouncements from day to day, or from event to event; so their positions are subject to being discounted by the media as "old news" because they usually have not changed since they were initially or last reported.

A recent study tracks the effects of such coverage on voters' evaluations of the candidates, showing that the majority of these evaluations in January and February were based on personality.[13] This occurred presumably because of the news content to which the voters were exposed, though this was not tested directly. Of equal significance, however, is the shift in such evaluations over time; among those interviewed after the June primaries, issues were more important in their evaluations. It remains to be seen whether this cross-sectional shift can be attributed to changing emphases in the news or to a learning process that takes place during the primary and caucus period.

A second characteristic of campaign coverage is a pattern in the allocation

107

of space that corresponds to expectations of performance in the next scheduled event or with the order of finish in the last one. In the early phase of the process, the better-known, better-organized, and better-funded candidates get more coverage than those farther back in the pack. As the balloting begins, the media's "verdict"[14] is reflected in the allocation of space in accord with performance, tempered by results that conform to expectations.[15]

A third characteristic of the coverage is that a disproportionate amount is given to the early events, and relatively less coverage is devoted to the end of the schedule. This front loading meant that more than one-quarter (28 percent) of all the coverage of the primaries and caucuses between January and the last event in 1980 on CBS and in the UPI wire was devoted to Iowa and New Hampshire.[16] The voters in California, who participate on the last day of the primary schedule, have not had any effective role to play in presidential selection under the new rules. Their diminished status is reflected in the fact that "coverage per delegate at stake" is sixty times as great for the New Hampshire primary as it is for the California primary.

These patterns describe typical coverage and its effects on candidate recognition and momentum; yet catching the press off guard can have important benefits for candidates who exceed expectations. Nowhere was that more visible than in the quantity and quality of coverage of Senator Gary Hart in the early phase of the 1984 primary schedule after his "surprise showing" in the Iowa caucus. What is particularly significant about such performances and the coverage they engender is their effect on evaluations of candidates among voters who have had no other contact with them than news exposure. These evaluations were based upon individuals' comparisons of news coverage of Hart's success set against their personal stereotypes of what a successful politician is. The media provided the cues about Hart's success by more and better coverage, most of it highly personalized. He therefore came to be seen as hard working, trustworthy, and competent, because these are the traits a candidate must possess to achieve electoral success.

That evaluations of Hart changed in conjunction with his success is not surprising, of course. The significance of the shifts is that they came so rapidly and without direct contact between the candidate and the electorate either through campaign visits or through the controlled messages of his advertisements. It is also important to note that this effect was visible at the beginning of the nominating process when it was still relatively open. Front loading had something to do with the significance the media attached to these early results. This explains much of the difference between the Hart movement in 1984 and the challenge to President Jimmy Carter from Governor Jerry Brown of California in 1980. Brown's victories came too late, when perceptions of Carter's inevitable renomination were fixed and as coverage of the prenomination period was waning.

The Importance of Survey Research in Structuring Coverage

Survey research, or polling, has a long history in the media's coverage of American electoral politics. In the "old" system, this technique and the publication of results were primarily used in the general election campaign. The Gallup Poll appeared as a syndicated newspaper column in the 1930s, as did Archibald Crossley's work for the Hearst papers; Elmo Roper got his start at the same time with *Fortune*. When primaries and caucuses were less significant to the selection process, it was nevertheless possible to consult national surveys for readings on the relative standings of candidates among their party faithful as well as the results of hypothetical pairings of opposing candidates in "trial heats."

From the media's perspective, survey research contributes to "good" coverage because the quantified results suggest a measure of objectivity and precision. The survey questions that can be most easily asked and reported are about personal factors and strategic considerations, such as relative standing, rather than about issues, and they coincide with the media's predispositions about newsworthiness. The use of the telephone now provides extremely timely survey data. For the networks, the elite national press, and an increasing number of local outlets, surveys are now being conducted for the media as well as being reported by them. The proprietary nature of the data that results in copywritten stories is just as compelling a factor in explaining their increasing use as their newsworthy qualities.

In the case of the networks and their print partners, these survey data play another, less obvious role in *structuring* coverage as well as providing content. This is especially clear in the use of exit surveys conducted on primary and caucus days. Data available by midafternoon provide an important cue for scheduling interviews and structuring the format and content of postelection analysis. Gatekeepers' decisions in the media are informed by these survey results, particularly by those from the first half of the day's interviewing. Within the confines of a thirty-minute show or thirty column-inches of news space, these surveys can provide information for determining the lead, formulating questions for interviews, arranging the quotations from sources, and adding interpretation to the results.

Two important shifts in the use of survey material appeared in the coverage of the 1984 primary. The first was an early piece prepared by CBS News and the *New York Times* that tried to set the context of the Iowa caucus by comparing the state's electorate to the nation as a whole. Later in the spring, they used a panel study to look at shifts in preferences throughout the primary season and subsequently used an oversample of black respondents to assess the Jackson candidacy. Second, ABC News and the *Washington Post* began to use rolling cross-sections of respondents to track the candidates and

109

estimate shifts among voters in several early primary states as election day approached. This technique permitted a different and extremely relevant perspective on the dynamics of the nominating process, especially on the momentum of the Hart phenomenon. Unfortunately, the overwhelming emphasis in the reporting derived from these surveys was on these shifting relative standings of the candidates rather than on changes in the electorate's attention to issues or the ability of voters to distinguish the policy positions of the candidates.

The Special Status of Incumbents

Almost all of the literature on the media in American electoral politics stresses the advantages of incumbency.[17] Most of the literature addresses presidential elections.[18] One recent study provides a fresh perspective on the control an incumbent can exercise over the flow of coverage during the primary process, and a second suggests a new way of evaluating the quality of news coverage incumbents receive.

Kerbel used original source materials in the Gerald R. Ford Library to analyze patterns of media access to the White House, measured as "requests for interviews" granted.[19] Of particular interest are the interactions between the president and the press during spring 1976. The essence of the findings are that President Ford became more accessible generally; his interest shifted from "major" media outlets to local ones, with an increased use of both radio and group interview formats; and the requests granted were distributed geographically and over time in a way that could be predicted by the primary calendar.

These data suggest a number of factors in the relationship beetween incumbent presidents and the media that should be subjected to further scrutiny as equivalent source materials become available for the Carter and eventually for the Reagan presidencies. The shift toward increased local coverage is important because of other research that suggests that local media provide "softer" and more favorable coverage for officeholders than the national media.[20] The data also provide strong circumstantial evidence that "presidents as candidates" clearly understand the effect of quantity and quality of campaign coverage on electoral success and the advantage of targeting the local media to maximize this effect.

Iyengar, Peters, and Kinder conducted a series of experiments in which they manipulated the content of recorded network evening news shows to stimulate different reactions to the coverage of the president.[21] The essence of these effects is captured in the concept of "priming," the process by which network news programs call attention to only selected national issues and thereby significantly affect "the standards by which presidents are judged."[22] The application of criteria of newsworthiness in the selection of stories and in the way they are "played," in conjunction with the prominence of the evening news as an information source for most Americans, suggest the critical importance of network news broadcasts in the public's assessments of presidential performance.

The priming concept is a variation of "agenda setting" and explains how issues shift in importance to an audience as cues provided by the media change. The most obvious cues are story placement and length, and it is generally assumed that the president, above all other political figures, can generate coverage almost at will. This provides him, in principle, with a substantial advantage in adjusting the agenda to emphasize those issues on which he has performed well or which highlight his accomplishments. The concept of priming goes beyond agenda setting, however; it suggests that the "play" of the story on television will affect not only the dimensions of presidential evaluation but the valence (whether he is evaluated positively or negatively) of it as well.

If the effects of priming appear in the general election campaign, why would they not be a factor in the prenomination phase of the contest? To the extent that the quality of news coverge can be affected by the packaging of the president,[23] including control over both the topics to be emphasized and the format in which the president will appear, then some leverage can presumably be exerted on both the quantity, but more important, on the quality, of coverage that results. The initiation of new domestic programs and the scheduling of foreign travel or visitors during the primary period, for example, can provide an important framing device for the coverage of a president seeking reelection.

It is difficult to assess the significance of priming ex post facto for the primaries and caucuses of 1976, 1980, and 1984, when the incumbents began as clear favorites for renomination. The 1988 contest is potentially a more interesting venue in which to observe and evaluate the significance of priming for an incumbent vice-president seeking the nomination. Beyond providing a clue about the support George Bush might expect to receive from Ronald Reagan, his travel and speaking schedules between fall 1987 and summer 1988 will serve as a device for developing his stature and image through the control of his public appearances.[24] Incumbents who understand how the news is made and how it affects their public image can influence their treatment in the press and their evaluations by the electorate.

Intraparty Debates as Media Events

One other recent development in the media's changing role in the prenomination process deserves some consideration—the sponsorship and broadcast of intraparty debates of primary and caucus candidates. These have all of the characteristics of "media events" except that they are scheduled and arranged by the media in conjunction with the candidates. The advantages for many of the candidates, particularly when the events are scheduled early, is free exposure that can lead to increased recognition by the electorate. The advantages for the networks include limited exclusive coverage and guaranteed news content, even though the live audiences may be small. Informing the electorate is part of the special function of the news divisions that distinguishes them from their entertainment counterparts, and these events provide an opportunity to showcase the network "talent" as well.

Unfortunately, the secondary reporting of these events, which has a much larger audience, still does not add substantially to the coverage of issues. The compelling images of recent New Hampshire appearances, for example, include a contest over the microphone on the Republican side and a finger-pointing scene between John Glenn and Walter Mondale on the Democratic side. The importance of conflict as a criteria for selecting and framing stories is well understood, so it is not surprising that these images should prevail.

It is likely that we will see more of these joint appearances in the future, especially in 1988 when the nomination should be wide open in both parties. Recent experience suggests that one way such debates could increase discussion of issues is to devote at least some portion of the program to opportunities for the candidates to question one another. Their sense of the important differences between them is likely to focus on issues or policy, and their questions are likely to emphasize these differences. The reporting is still likely to emphasize who did well and who did poorly, and how each candidate's performance affected his or her standing in the electorate; but more coverage will likely be given to issues and policy than if only reporters and commentators get to ask the questions.

Conclusions

In the absence of strong party machines that inform and mobilize the electorate, the news media have become increasingly important in the prenomination phase of the presidential selection process. From one perspective—applying the criteria of newsworthiness to large, multicandidate fields—it can be argued that they are now the essential institutional force in the process. Through both the quantity and the quality of press coverage the candidates receive, critical judgments are fashioned by political elites, likely voters, and other less active members of the electorate. These include decisions about contributing time and money as well as about whether to vote and for whom.

Campaigns develop momentum from the successful implementation of a strategy based upon building recognition, working toward positive evaluation, and thereby influencing the way their success is reported in the media. Expectations established in the media must be met or exceeded for a candidate to be classified as a "front-runner." The only hope for a candidate farther back in the pack is to catch the media unaware, a task that is becoming increasingly difficult as the press's scrutiny of the process intensifies.

The front loading of the coverage and the disproportionate amount devoted to the early primaries provide important clues about what might be expected if attempts to shorten the prenomination period are successful. On the one hand, the relative advantages of front-runners will be greater in a truncated primary season lasting only four to eight weeks. Covering a shortened primary and caucus campaign with national or regional surveys in conjunction with standard reportorial techniques, the media will be inclined to produce stories with more content about strategy and emphasis on horse race journalism. On the other hand, candidates who are unable to make a strong showing early will be discarded sooner.

Certain elements of current coverage will have to be rethought and redefined in the context of a shorter campaign period. More extensive background reporting on the candidates will be required because emphasis by candidates and critics on the media's information role will increase. A truncated primary and caucus schedule will demand more comparative reporting. Emphasis will likely shift to regional coverage, with consequences for covering the special interests of electorates with geographically based needs and policy demands. One benefit of this could be an increase in the coverage of issues.

Such a trend could signal increased importance for polls conducted by or for the media. The appropriate use of survey research techniques—based upon simultaneous regional and national samples and the comparisons that could be made between them—could support such a shift in coverage. It would, however, require more complex research designs, perhaps a better-trained cohort of political reporters or simply more expert consultation, and a different style of presentation of the findings. One consequence could be stories that deal with the dynamics of candidate recognition, evaluation, and preference in the electorate. This is not a story line that could be organized and sustained throughout a four- or five-month calendar, but it may prove more feasible for two or three months. It is more likely to be suited to print reporting than to television journalism.

Another likely consequence of a shortened primary and caucus calendar will be a demand for more joint appearances by candidates, organized around the revised schedule. Perhaps this trend toward debates is an inevitable result of television's increasing news role, but it will almost certainly be accelerated in a shortened prenomination period. A critical issue will be who will control the setting and the format. If the political parties obtain and maintain control, it is likely that the number of candidates participating will be greater and the issue content higher. If the media gain control, recent experience suggests that the events will become more of a showcase for network talent, will be subject to greater restrictions on candidate participation, especially early in the process, and will focus relatively less on issues.

None of these factors suggests a diminished role for the media in the contemporary nominating process, only a different one. The name of the game, from the candidate's perspective, is still recognition, positive evaluation, and momentum. The symbiotic relationship between candidates and reporters is unlikely to change under any of the current proposals for revision of the system. One important criterion for evaluating alternative reform proposals is whether they will result in more coverage of issues in the campaign and contribute to a better-informed electorate, or only accentuate the media's current preoccupation with horse race journalism.

Notes

1. For the purposes of this analysis, the term "media" refers to the news media and the dissemination of information that is relatively uncontrolled by candidates. These messages are distinguished from those carried in the candidates' advertisements, which are highly controlled.

2. Donald Matthews, "'Winnowing': The News Media and the 1976 Presidential Nominations," in James D. Barber, ed., *Race for the Presidency* (Englewood Cliffs, N.J.: Prentice-Hall, Inc.), pp. 55-78.

3. Doris A. Graber, *Mass Media and American Politics*, 2d ed. (Washington, D.C.: CQ Press, 1984), pp. 77-79.

4. Daniel J. Boorstin, *The Image: or What Happened to the American Dream.* (New York: Atheneum, 1962), pp. 7-44.

5. Michael J. Robinson, "The Media in 1980: Was the Message the Message?" in Austin Ranney, ed., *The American Elections of 1980* (Washington, D.C.: American Enterprise Institute, 1981), pp. 171-211.

6. Carl P. Leubsdorf, "The Reporter and the Presidential Candidate," *Annals of the American Academy of Political and Social Science*, vol. 427 (September 1976), pp. 1-11.

7. William C. Adams, "Media Coverage of Campaign '84: A Preliminary Report," *Public Opinion*, vol. 7, no. 2 (April/May 1984), pp. 9-13.

8. Thomas R. Marshall, "The News Verdict and Public Opinion During the Primaries," in William C. Adams, ed., *Television Coverage of the 1980 Presidential Campaign* (Norwood, N.J.: Ablex, 1983), pp. 49-67.

9. See, Peter Clarke and Susan Evans, *Covering Campaigns: Journalism in Congressional Elections* (Stanford, Calif.: Stanford University Press, 1983); Thomas E. Patterson, *The Mass Media Election: How Americans Choose Their President* (New York: Praeger, 1980); and Michael J. Robinson and Margaret Sheehan, *Over the Wire and on TV: CBS and UPI in Campaign '80* (New York: Russel Sage Foundation, 1983).

10. F. Christopher Arterton, *Media Politics: The News Strategies of Presidential Campaigns* (Lexington, Mass.: D.C. Heath, 1984).

11. See, Patterson, *Mass Media Election;* Robinson and Sheehan, *Over the Wire*; Adams, "Media Coverage"; David Hoffman, "At Home: The Candidate, Packaged and Protected," *Washington Journalism Review*, September 1984, pp. 37-41; and

Michael J. Robinson, "The Media in Campaign '84: Part II—Wingless, Toothless, and Hopeless," *Public Opinion*, vol. 8, no. 1 (February/March 1985), pp. 43-48.

12. Robinson and Sheehan, *Over the Wire*, p. 163.

13. Thomas R. Marshall, "Evaluating Presidential Nominees: Opinion Polls, Issues, and Personalities," *Western Political Quarterly*, vol.36, no. 4 (December 1983), pp. 650-59.

14. Thomas R. Marshall, *Presidential Nominations in a Reform Age* (New York: Praeger, 1981).

15. Adams, "Media Coverage," p. 10.

16. Robinson and Sheehan, *Over the Wire*, pp. 174-78.

17. Robinson would be the significant exception to this generalization, but perhaps the addition of 1984 to his interpretive database would cause him to adjust his perspective.

18. Examples are: Benjamin I. Page, *Choices and Echoes in Presidential Elections* (Chicago, Ill.: University of Chicago Press, 1978); Michael B. Grossman and Martha J. Kumar, *Portraying the President: The White House and the News Media* (Baltimore, Md.: Johns Hopkins University Press, 1981); Shanto Iyengar, Mark D. Peters, and Donald R. Kinder, "Experimental Demonstrations of the 'Not-So-Minimal' Consequences of Television News Programs," *American Political Science Review*, vol. 76 (1982), pp. 848-58; and Shanto Iyengar and Donald R. Kinder, "More Than Meets the Eye: TV News, Priming, and Public Evaluations of the President," in George Comstock, ed., *Public Communication and Behavior* (New York: Academic Press, forthcoming).

Assessments of nonpresidential elections can be found in: Clarke and Evans, *Covering Campaigns*; and Edie N. Goldenberg and Michael W. Traugott, *Campaigning for Congress* (Washington, D.C.: CQ Press, 1984).

19. Matthew R. Kerbel, "Against the Odds: Media Access in the Administration of President Gerald Ford" Paper delivered at the Annual Meeting of the Midwest Political Science Association, Chicago, Illinois, April 1984.

20. Michael J. Robinson, "Three Faces of Congressional Media," in Thomas E. Mann and Norman J. Ornstein, eds., *The New Congress* (Washington, D.C.: American Enterprise Institute, 1981), pp. 55-96.

21. Iyengar, Peters, and Kinder, "Experimental Demonstrations."

22. Iyengar and Kinder, "More Than Meets the Eye," (in manuscript).

23. Hoffman, "At Home," p. 37.

24. This possibility has already been suggested using different terminology, in a recent column by David Broder, "The Heir Implicit: Bush Finds Himself in a Strengthened Position for '88," *Washington Post Weekly Edition*, vol. 2, no. 23 (April 8, 1985), p. 6.

A New Primary System

Charles T. Manatt

We are here not only to reflect on the past but to set a direction for the future on one of the most vital questions of our political system—the way we choose our presidents. Except for prescribing the time of the election and the function of the electoral college, the Constitution is remarkably silent on this question. There is not a single word about political parties or nominating methods; there was no provision even for the separate election of the president and the vice president until Aaron Burr nearly tricked Thomas Jefferson out of his victory of 1800. The framers had George Washington consciously in mind as their first president, and they seem almost unconsciously to have treated him as the model for all future elections—someone who could emerge as a consensus choice, on the basis of past service and not of partisan appeals.

Events swiftly confounded any such expectation. Madison and Hamilton, who had decried factions in *The Federalist Papers*, soon joined others in founding opposing political parties. Each sought the presidency in different years; one succeeded, and the other failed.

For nearly two centuries since then we have invented, amended, blamed, and praised the means of picking presidential nominees. We have moved from King Caucus to what we regard as an open process, where voters are supposed to have a direct and decisive say. The present period of change began, in a sense, in 1936, when Franklin Roosevelt in effect commanded the Democratic convention to repeal the two-thirds rule, which had nearly denied him the nomination four years before. The immediate effect was to deprive the southern states of their traditional veto power. The longer-range result was to foster the idea that convention rules—once thought to be a sacrosanct part of an implicit yet delicately balanced compact or an inviolate matter of states' rights—could be reformulated or "reformed" at will, at the national level.

After the 1936 convention, however, nothing of great consequence changed in the rules for more than three decades. I suspect the reason was the tendency of the parties to nominate the most popular candidates. When, arguably, they failed to do so—for example, in the Stevenson-Kefauver contest of 1952— the contestants represented no fundamental cleavage of issues or ideology within the party, and the supporters of the loser soon rallied to the winner. That same year such a cleavage did perhaps exist among Republicans, but who could persuasively contend that Dwight Eisenhower was not the choice of the people and therefore was and had to be the nominee of a rigged or unfair convention?

Yet pressures related more to the emerging civil rights movement than to the identity of any particular nominee were building beneath the surface and would augment the coming wave of reform. Democratic conventions hotly debated whether to require "loyalty oaths"—pledges in advance to support the national ticket—as a condition of seating delegates. In 1964 the Mississippi Freedom Democratic Party challenged the regular Mississippi delegation, and the compromise settlement negotiated by the young attorney general of Minnesota, Walter Mondale, put the national party squarely into the business of regulating delegate selection in the state of Mississippi.

The precedents and pressures were there, and the 1968 convention provided the spark that set off a chain reaction of reform that has not yet spent itself. In 1968 there was an impression, right or wrong, that the eventual nominee, Hubert Humphrey, who had not entered a single primary, was not the popular choice. The critics could point to some glaring examples of apparent unfairness: a Georgia delegation picked personally by the governor, with no democratic participation or recourse; a Texas delegation with the unit rule, forcing the opponents of the Vietnam War within that delegation to cast a vote in favor of it; other delegations selected far in advance of the convention, long before the campaigns of Robert Kennedy and Eugene McCarthy and even longer before the withdrawal of Lyndon Johnson.

Added to these pressures was the rising call for the empowerment of new forces—with blacks now joined by Hispanics, the young, and women, who were starting to express a new and powerful consciousness of their own identity. To conciliate these forces and as part of the effort to rescue his candidacy from the chaos of the Chicago convention, Humphrey agreed to establish a commission to rewrite the rules for 1972 and beyond.

This history points to an important insight: the reforms were not an accident but a result of irrepressible events and broader trends. It also suggests that although the rules can be—and have been—repeatedly amended, the reforms cannot, in their fundamental aspects, be rolled back. The Republican party, which was not the crucible of these changes, has adopted many of them. One reason is that state laws that apply to both parties were adopted to accommodate the Democratic reforms. The other reason, more pervasive and powerful, is that the rules changes reflected real changes in American society—changes that either party could ignore only at its peril. At the 1984 Dallas convention, Republicans denounced quotas—and then celebrated the fact that nearly half their delegates were women.

There are two fashionable reactions to this period of reform, both of

117

which I reject. I do not accept the notion that the old system produced better nominees and somehow did so precisely because of its rules. Any such argument depends on selective history and on the assumption that the nominating process can be made into a special preserve, sealed off from the mood and movements of the times. The old system produced Harding and Nixon as well as Eisenhower and Kennedy. We Democrats had fewer chances to make mistakes in those years not because the rules protected us but because the unprecedented four terms of Franklin Roosevelt prevented us for a long time from nominating someone else. Who imagines that the old rules could have survived the transformation of modern communications and consciousness? After Watergate could the Republicans—or the Democrats—really have chosen their nominee in a smoke-filled room? If the choice in 1984 had been left to party leaders and not to primaries, would it have been any different, given that so many of those leaders had already decided by the end of 1983 to endorse Mondale?

Just as I reject the notion that the old was better, I also reject the fashionable argument that what we have now is good enough and that it cannot or should not be improved. Revisions in the rules will not, on our side, cure all that ails the Democratic party or, on the other side, alter the underlying factors that could undermine the present Republican success. But revisions can make the system more rational, less beholden to separate groups, and more reflective of the national will.

This is not only an appropriate time to act; it also presents a nearly unique opportunity for change. In 1988, for the first time in twenty-eight years, neither party will have an incumbent president eligible for reelection. Together both parties can shape and seek changes based on merit and not on the calculus of individual interest. They can move in Congress, in ways that I will outline, to mandate steps toward goals that virtually everyone professes but no one so far seems able to achieve.

The critical cause of our failure to achieve them is that we have considered the question chiefly in the context of party commissions, which have largely been dominated by the representatives and adherents of prospective candidates. Congress offers a different forum, which can focus on broader purposes and can invoke effective powers of enforcement. Congressional action not only is the best way to deal with the length of the process but may be the only way. Federal legislation can deny matching funds to candidates who violate federal guidelines.

Those guidelines should set primaries on four dates—the first or second Tuesdays in March, April, May, and June. Caucuses could be held any time in the week following the primaries. To avoid the distortion of having all the states in a single region vote on the same day, without the balancing effect of a more representative diversity, Congress should consider time-zone primaries. Which time zone went first and which followed in any given year should be determined by lottery. For the 1988 campaign, the lottery should be held in December 1986. Any candidate who participated in a nonapproved delegate selection process held outside this system would lose federal matching funds.

As a former national chairman, I saw what happened when we tried, on our own, to shorten the process for 1984. We made some progress—Iowa came five weeks later than in 1980 and New Hampshire a week later—but it proved virtually impossible to do more, especially to eliminate the special status of the two states. At least one candidate will always parade as their defender, and the others cannot afford to be seen as the ones who tried to deny Iowa or New Hampshire its rightful priority. So those states can pick their dates, regardless of party rules, and assume that by the time the convention comes, the winning candidate will not let it refuse to seat their delegates. Imagine the plight of candidates who had to campaign in the New Hampshire primary after trying to abolish it. The issue would not be the economy, or Central America, or new ideas, or old values. It would be why they tried to deprive the state of its place in the news and its lion's share of campaign revenues.

This is no way to pick a president. In 1984 candidates had to pay, according to a price list, to put up banners or posters at a New Hampshire party event. They even had to pay a price to speak. Perhaps there is a rough justice in that, at least for some political speakers we have all heard; but such practices degrade not only the candidates but the process. They do not advance the cause of picking a nominee; they exploit it.

New Hampshire makes no more sense as the first primary for selecting a Democratic nominee than Massachusetts would as the first primary for the Republicans. And although I was raised in Iowa and I will certainly hear about this when I go back, Iowa too has no special claim and deserves no automatic priority.

The system I suggest has the added advantage of inviting a more coherent and less debilitating dialogue. In 1983 and 1984 we saw an increasing pro-liferation of joint appearances, debates, and speech contests, often used by state parties as fund-raising vehicles. Too readily these events tempt candidates, especially those who are behind, to launch the kind of attacks that can almost fatally weaken a likely nominee for the coming campaign. What we need is a greater certainty of debates in the general election and greater control over the number and intensity of exchanges during the primary period. Perhaps, as part of the reform I have proposed, the national parties should sponsor four debates in 1988—on the four Saturdays or Sundays before the designated primary dates.

Any plan to shorten the process will be only half successful if it fails to deal with the straw polls, which foster an early start and a relentlessly paced campaign. Here, again, I believe that the matching funds system provides a mechanism for reform. The law should be amended so that any contributions raised before October 1 in the year preceding the primaries will not be eligible for federal matching. Candidates could raise enough to sustain a preprimary operation, but they would be unlikely to raise more and more unmatchable money to compete in unsanctioned straw polls.

To me October 1 is certainly a reasonable date to start matching. A quarter of a century ago, John Kennedy was counted as an early entry because he announced his candidacy on January 3, 1960, and the crucial organizing meeting of his campaign was held in October 1959. Perhaps we cannot restore that sense of proportion to the process; but at least we can moderate a situation in which we are perilously close to the moment when, in Adlai Stevenson's words, the nominee will be "the last survivor." The precondition of running for president should not be that a candidate is out of office or has to neglect totally, for two or three years, the office he or she may already hold.

The other major problem, the other perennial complaint about the system, is its cost. Frankly, I do not believe we will find a way to nominate presidents on the cheap. But we can find a way to reduce the dominance of fund raising in campaigns. One step I have already discussed is to limit matching for 1987 to contributions given after October 1, 1987. At the same time we should raise the limit on an individual contribution to $2,000, and we should match the first $1,000 rather than just the first $250.

There is no reason to hold candidates hostage to limits set a decade ago that are worth only half as much in real dollars today. And there is no reason to make it progressively harder to raise money, to make candidates allocate more and more of their time to searching out contributors, simply so that they will have barely resources enough to compete in the first primaries.

Yet wouldn't an October 1 date for matching have precisely the opposite effect, forcing candidates to put greater energy into fund raising later in the process? They could, however, gather pledges in advance; they could draw up budgets. All this rule says is that they could not actually receive—or spend—contributions before October 1 if they wanted to see that money matched.

In closing, let me reaffirm my belief that, in the truest sense, we can reform the primary process only if we reach beyond traditional candidate rivalries and across the usual partisan divisions. Republicans and Democrats in Congress can bring about changes that, separately, the Republican and Democratic national committees can probably never achieve.

In that spirit, let us meet the challenges before us—whether they affect the way we nominate presidents or the way we conduct our national debates on the great issues. Let us work with one another where we can, disagree when we must, and set a high standard of civility and mutual respect. In short, let us remember the plain majesty of Gerry Ford's inaugural message—

that no matter how vigorous the debate between us, it is really "just a little straight talk among friends"; that the bond between us, "though strained, is unbroken"; and that, most of all, it depends on "instincts of openness and candor."

Part Three

Summary,
Colloquy,
and
Recommendations

The Rapporteur's Summary

William Schneider

I have the happy but difficult task of summarizing the contemplations of this group of great minds. We have heard all points of view at our sessions. I think this is a group that may know too much to give sharp, decisive prescriptions.

Can we predict what would happen if there were a national primary, or regional primaries on four specific dates? A great philosopher, Casey Stengel, once said, "Never make predictions, especially about the future." We are mostly social scientists, and, as we know, the business of social scientists is to predict the past—and we do not always get even that right. Alternatively, we could make the sort of predictions professional politicians do—clear, decisive, and often wrong.

Let us look at the Democratic party. The Democratic party nominated Hubert Humphrey. Then it formed the McGovern-Fraser Commission, which had a very clear mandate to rewrite the party rules so there would be no more Hubert Humphreys. The party instituted more primaries and opened up the process.

The Democrats nominated George McGovern the next time. A lot of people did not like that, however; so the rules were again revised, with a clear mandate: no more George McGoverns.

Next the Democratic party nominated Jimmy Carter, who won the election. But that did not work out terribly well; so the party formed the Hunt Commission, which gave party professionals and elected officials more of a say in the decision. The mandate was: no more Jimmy Carters.

The result of that process was the nomination of Walter Mondale. We now have a Fairness Commission, which may try to outlaw superdelegates and change the process once again. The Fairness Commission was formed as a concession to the losing candidates in 1984, Gary Hart and Jesse Jackson. It, too, has a clear mandate: no more Walter Mondales.

That is the way the professionals do it.

I think we would agree with Charles Manatt that two things are not true. One is that the old system worked just fine. We know from the many accounts we have heard at this meeting that that is not true. It is also not true that the new system works just fine. As President Ford said in the opening session, he sensed a popular discontent, a feeling that the process is far too long and far too expensive.

Alexander Heard pointed out that the motive for reform is never abstract, remote, detached, or objective, that all efforts for change have unspoken assumptions behind them. I think that is the case here at this conference. The assumption is that we want pragmatic, professional, experienced leadership capable of appealing to a broad consensus in the party, if not in the nation. Martin Wattenberg pointed out that, while the first choice of the rank and file in a party usually gets the nomination, the candidate with the broadest range of support does not always, or even typically, win. We at this conference have a bias against ideological factions, against single-issue groups and their influence in politics, and against the rule of inexperience.

Terry Sanford reminded us of the defects of the present system: it requires full-time campaigning and so rules out most active officeholders, and it gives power to organized minorities, one-issue groups, and extreme wings of our parties. Most important is the loss of the representative or deliberative function of the delegates. The candidates pick the delegates who pick the candidates, and the convention is reduced to an electoral college. Governor Sanford suggested that candidates who participate in unsanctioned functions be in some way penalized, for example, that their names not be allowed to be placed in nomination. That is an interesting idea. Mr. Manatt suggested that a stronger sanction be used, namely, that candidates who violate the rules lose their claim to federal matching funds.

Theodore Lowi gave us some important insights into the history of the nominating process, which, he said, is intrinsically connected to the system of government. A mass plebiscitary democracy has replaced the system of party democracy. The new system means a strong, discretionary president who has a direct relationship with the voters. Professor Lowi said that the reforms in the nominating process did not cause the transformation of presidential leadership but simply accelerated it. He suggested that a fundamental change in the nominating process requires a change in the regime. We must somehow deflate presidential government if we are to make any basic change. We cannot very easily go back, but we can improve.

In his review of the data on presidential elites, Warren Miller pointed to some good things and some bad things about the people who now choose our presidents. One of the good things is that the party elites have sharpened their differences. The parties are more polarized, and they may be approaching a model of responsible party government, with clearly defined differences between the parties.

There are, of course, also bad things, including the occasionally wide gaps between the delegates and the rank and file, most notably for the Democrats in 1972 and the Republicans in 1980.

Professor Miller also said that the internal contests for leadership within the party override institutional changes and changes in the rules. That is a key point. The rules did not cause most of the significant changes in the parties that we have been reviewing. The New Politics Democrats and New Right Republicans emerged for substantive reasons and, in many cases, changed the rules afterwards. Professor Miller has performed the valuable task of keeping our causal arrows pointed in the right direction.

Martin Wattenberg reviewed the role of political parties in our process. He pointed out that the process destroys the unity of our parties. The party that shows the greatest division in the process usually loses.

I would add that every incumbent president from 1964 to 1980 was challenged for renominaton. This is a new pattern, and it promotes the worst kind of disunity in our parties.

A quotation I found recently in a newspaper illustrates our party problem. Talking about the Democratic party in his state, the Speaker of the California Assembly said, "The Democratic party is not relevant. Those of us in office do not rely on it. Instead, we cultivate our own voters, do our own fund raising and our own candidate development." When reminded of some differences he had with the Democratic state chairwoman because of some remarks she had made about the chief justice of the California Supreme Court, he said, "I treat her like I treat most chairpeople. I'm not going to waste time with the party. My job is to meet the needs of forty-seven egomaniacs who make up my majority in the state Assembly. Of course, where I can be of assistance to the party, I will." I think that speaks volumes about where parties have ended up in our political system.

Professor Wattenberg said that the media, through their distorted coverage, have in fact reinstated winner-take-all primaries. I think that is true. He suggested a series of reforms for consideration. Approval voting is one possibility. Another is to allow the first runner-up for the nomination the right of first refusal for vice-president. Most provocative is the notion that a national primary might be preceded by an endorsement convention, which would allow the candidates to get name recognition before the primary.

That is already done in some states, including New York. The candiates compete for the endorsement of the Democratic convention. The losing candidate immediately labels the endorsed candidate the candidate of the bosses, and that becomes an effective campaign issue. That is what happened with the AFL-CIO presidential endorsement in 1983. Gary Hart competed just as hard as everyone else for that endorsement. When he lost it, he used it as an issue against Walter Mondale, who instantly became the candidate of the labor bosses and the party establishment.

Voters see nuisances in the system, but Robert Teeter noted that the voters had few objections about its essential nature or the candidates it produces. Warren Miller added that dissatisfaction with the system comes mostly from supporters of candidates who lose.

In his presentation on the media, Michael Traugott described the symbiotic relationship that has developed between candidates and reporters. Both he and David Mathews described the press as the mediating structure that has replaced parties. The press, Professor Traugott argued, has a serious problem in its coverage. It is preoccupied with strategy and horse race journalism, rather than with issues or policy. Werner Veit added that that is not by choice; strategy is what there is to cover, although he would rather spend his money covering other things.

The press plays a critical role in the process. It produces the commodities all candidates want, namely, name recognition and momentum. Those who are not the front-runners have the unenviable task of trying to catch the media unaware. Some, like John Anderson, are skillful at this game; they go before a group like the gun owners' association and say "I am for gun control," or before the farmers in Iowa and say "I am for the grain embargo." Anderson played to the press in this way and did a very nice job of it.

The press, Professor Traugott said, is constantly looking for a lead. He presented some interesting observations about the misuse of poll data for that purpose: it is used not necessarily to inform the electorate but to guide coverage and to allow editors and reporters to see quickly how they should formulate their stories. Professor Traugott suggested that media-based polls should be improved by using better-trained political reporters and, as a disinterested academic, he called for more expert consultation.

Michael Malbin described the pernicious effects of the current contribution and spending limits, which lengthen campaigns and require campaign managers to be devious in looking for ways around those limits. Mr. Malbin said the present contribution limits are totally inadequate for the job candidates must do under the present delegate-selection system. Limits, he said, should fit the delegate-selection system we now have. The candidates are simply not getting adequate funds for their campaigns.

Mr. Malbin's prescription was either to raise the contribution limits and possibly let national spending limits equal the sum of the state spending limits or simplify the process. If we do not want to raise that much money, we should not require candidates to go through such a long and tedious process.

Mr. Manatt echoed some of those recommendations. He suggested that we establish a later starting date for eligibility for matching funds, that we raise contribution limits and matching requirements ($1,000 was the figure he used), and that we end the out-of-date spending limits.

Xandra Kayden described the purpose of the campaign finance law as that of controlling the power of the special interests. She pointed out that only in some ways has it succeeded. The law has taken big business out of the nominating process and curbed the excesses of some interests. It has also created a certain degree of professionalism in the fund-raising process. The effect in presidential campaigns has been to devalue interest-group giving and to raise the value of membership organizatons, such as labor, which can donate services as well as money.

Dr. Kayden also felt that the system has stimulated the rise of independent spending by groups of the New Right that use their technology to balance the influence of labor. In discussion about the connection between the New Right and the Republican party, Dr. Kayden pointed out that a high proportion of independent expenditures in 1984 did come from the New Right and went overwhelmingly to Republican candidates.

She also described a shift in independent spending to a period earlier in the process, mostly before the general election campaign. Dr. Kayden pointed to several problems with this kind of spending: those raising such funds make negative appeals, are not politically accountable for their statements, and are "wild cards" on the issues, operating outside the campaign. The obstacle to reforming that part of the process is the First Amendment and the Supreme Court's interpretation of it.

Neil Staebler offered several proposals to regulate independent expenditures, among them the requirement that the media offer free rebuttal time to candidates who are attacked. Michael Malbin pointed out that that will cost the media money, and they may not be enthusiastic about it. Limiting the content of independent expenditures to ideas and notifying candidates and the Federal Election Commission of all independent expenditure activities were also suggested.

Michael Nelson offered a spirited and eloquent defense of the current nominating system. He argued that reforms have not weakened the parties, that the decline of party strength started before the reforms, and that in recent years, the parties have revived even after the reforms were implemented. I think this is consistent with Warren Miller's presentation.

Mr. Nelson argued that the quality of presidents cannot be attributed to the rules. Both the old and the new processes provided us with leadership. He felt that the current system tests the skills a president must have—persuasion, self-presentation, and coalition-building. I am reminded of a book by Sidney Blumenthal, *The Permanent Campaign*, which describes the need for a president, even when governing, to fashion for himself a kind of permanent campaign. Those skills are well honed in our current nominating system.

Mr. Nelson then addressed the legitimacy of the present system to the voters. He called this the weakest aspect of the process because the voters are turned off by its complexity. Other commentators, however, including Robert Teeter, Warren Miller, and myself, presented arguments to refute this. The voters are turned off by many features of the system, but it is resoundingly populist in its essential characteristics.

129

Thomas Mann suggested changes he felt might be needed in our current system. He presented the possibilities for change as four options. The first option is to make no changes at all, which is more or less what Mr. Nelson recommended.

The second option is to go back, allowing more autonomy for state parties and greater involvement by party elites. David Mathews pointed out that any proposal seen as advancing party or professional power at the expense of public participation would not be feasible. The only possible reforms are those on which the public and party professionals agree. That makes the return to anything like the earlier system quite unlikely.

The third option is to standardize and rationalize the current system. Regional or time zone primaries (the so-called Udall plan, which many speakers brought up) and primaries confined to four specific dates, were two suggestions for rationalizing the system. Mr. Manatt's proposal that candidates who engage in unsanctioned activities should not receive matching funds could be part of this option. Another rationalizing reform would be a change in the campaign finance law raising the contribution limits and spending limits. The third option therefore would remove inefficiencies and inconsistencies and would standardize the current nominating system while preserving its many good features.

The fourth option is the most radical—to move toward a national primary, possibly with a preprimary convention or a 40 percent threshold requiring a runoff. This is the most extreme option, but Tom Mann pointed out that it has the virtue of being simple and allowing for less distortion or mediation by the press. The problem with this option, he said, is that everyone but the public is against it. He tried to tempt us into accepting the risk of a national primary by raising some provocative questions. Why, for instance, should we have a system that protects the interests of dark horses? Will a national primary really destroy our political parties? Would they not find other things to do?

Among participants at this conference, option three appears to have the most support: standardizing the current system, rationalizing it, removing its inefficiencies, while preserving many of its important and functional features.

I will conclude with an important comment made by Robert Finch. Drawing on the effect of Watergate in reforming campaign finances, he said that only a crisis or scandal is likely to produce the political momentum necessary to create a uniform federal election law.

Mr. President, those are the main findings and observations of this convocation.

Individual Commentary
and
Group Recommendations

Compiled and Edited by
George Grassmuck

Philip Converse: "Alex, I believe we are going to have some questions subsequently, right?"

Alexander Heard: "If there is wit in the multitude we will."

In the colloquy of the conference, many ideas about changing and improving the prenomination process were proposed, introduced for discussion, and often opposed. The careful preparations and the experience in presidential politics shared by all discussants supported the analysis that typified the two days of deliberations. The sessions were serious but not somber, and the product of the conference was hardly a complete platform of recommendations and pledges. Rather, after a few agreements and more disagreements, all in good humor, the invitees adjourned knowing they had again discussed a topic frequenlty analyzed. They left it a tender but not sore subject for further treatment in the near future. In short, this gathering opened the discussions that precede every presidential election, but provided careful thought and conclusions based upon the best available analyses and the most recent informative Democratic and Republican experiences.

PRESIDENT FORD set the tone for the conference when he opened it by saying, "Whenever I talk about this subject before any group, I always start by saying in my opinion the nomination process for the presidency takes too long and costs too much money. When I say that, there is immediate applause. It is the absolute consensus wherever I have made that statement."

ALEXANDER HEARD participated in opening the conference by noting the

131

timeliness of the topic as well as the frequency of its study. He stated that more than two hundred books on presidential selection had appeared in the past fifteen years and that several dozen analyses are now underway. History shows that change is the essence of the presidential nominating process and that change has several causes. Altered political interests are seen as a cause. The nation's characteristics and resulting popular expectations bring change in the presidential nominating procedures. Rapidity does as well, whether in mobility, in occupational transition, or in communications. Then too, said Chancellor Heard, unpredictability is ever present. "I would like to call it the law of unintended consequences that applies in political reform. Human beings are both complex and resourceful, and political institutions are subject to many external interventions as well as difficulties of design."

He stressed the need for being explicit about the goals and values the conference would recognize as well as about the measures to be recommended.

TERRY SANFORD, former governor of North Carolina, said the present nomination rules and resulting system prevent governors from running for the presidency. "Today one can say with certainty that the present Democratic nominating rules, and for that matter the Republican rules, essentially disqualify the governor of any state."

Because of the delegate selection rules, which the Democratic party initiated after 1968, rules that the Republican party follows to an extent, any sitting governor is out of the game. The reforms demand almost full-time campaigning for two years. Three years would be even better. In addition, because we rely so much on the primaries for final choice, we have "put tremendous power in the hands of organized minorities, or one-issue groups, or extreme wings of either party."

Governor Sanford cited the number of party chairmen who said his or her state party was not represented by the state's delegation to the national convention, and that returning delegates could not rationalize the nominating procedure in which they participated. This conference should seek ways to strengthen the political parties and ways to find capable leaders for the parties. Delegates chosen by the states to attend the national convention must be of high quality. They must be able to confer and to deliberate when they meet there to choose the best candidates within the party for the highest office.

The primary system is not expected to disappear, but it must be limited. That does not mean we should have a national primary; we should not. Nor should there be regional primaries, because regionalism would be unduly stressed. The states should, however, hold their primaries within a few months on acceptable dates. Before those months, straw polls and other like maneuvers should be discouraged by party regulations. "Basically," concluded Governor Sanford, "the parties need to save themselves. And the first step is to return to a rational plan for nominating presidential candidates, for doing what parties are best organized to do and essentially must do, facilitate the rise of leadership within the party."

One might expect from this conference strong recommendations for major changes in the presidential nomination process. To paraphrase Justice Oliver Wendell Holmes, however, great conferences over hard cases make few radical proposals. The discussions that followed each presentation, summarized in the following section of this chapter, gave hints that this gathering would work true to form; the reports of the three discussion groups that sought consensus on recommendations for change, summarized in the last section, also confirmed the aphorism.

Three major interests characterized the participants' presentations and recommendations. The first is proposed major changes in the general prenomination process. The second is the cost in dollars of running for nomination and the place of contributions as well as of donors in the process. The third is the participation or lack of it by parties, interest groups, states, and the millions of voters, many of whom show little interest.

What follows is, first, a distillation of the participants' discursive observations, which were always relevant and usually pertinent to each of the three topics. Following the commentary is a summary of the group recommendations for each of the three concerns: change, cost and contribution, and public involvement.

Individual Commentary

ALTERNATIVES TO THE PRESENT SYSTEM

PAUL KIRK speculated that we are in need of "a mechanism by which a candidate or candidates can earn the political and intellectual respect of the American people, and the right to govern their business." Ideas should be developed that bring a sense of order to the process as well as a little more civility to the debate. Unless the Democratic and the Republican parties address the matter together, "it may be that one or the other party will be over on one side of the aisle tinkering with the rules again."

He recognized the current advocacy of regional primaries, but hesitated to accept that change. He saw advantage, particularly for those candidates who are not well known and well financed, in using a small state, like South Carolina, "in which one could acquire a threshold visibility and spend some time working with the voters in a smaller media market." A threshold test would allow a candidate to acquire the momentum and attention needed for competing for name recognition and financial support. A regional primary would be too large and too costly for the unknown candidate.

Kirk noted that the Democratic party's Fairness Commission will consider

133

changes made before the 1984 convention in party rules, and he anticipated that other issues will be addressed, among them changes in the calendar and perhaps regional primaries.

HAMILTON JORDAN warned against spending much time, effort, and political capital trying to refine the present system. "As a Democrat it scares me to death to think my party would spend its time over the next three or four years trying to refine the process instead of looking at the fact that we lack a national message, or relevant national message." He saw the present procedure as already deliberative, open, and fair.

AUSTIN RANNEY recalled his adventures as an active participant in Democratic party reform efforts. He said reforms often have unanticipated consequences, so in proposing changes the conference should weigh "not only what is likely to be the effectiveness of a means to produce a particular end, but what side effects it might possibly have."

As an example, the McGovern-Fraser Commission sought to make the Democratic convention more open and more fair and to give everybody a chance to participate. This change would avoid the adoption of a national primary, the commission believed. "Somewhat to our consternation between 1968 and 1972, no fewer than fifteen states adopted new presidential primaries. We went from about a third of the delegates being selected by state primaries to more than two-thirds being selected, and the figure rose to as high as 75 percent selected by primaries." That was neither anticipated nor desired.

After other examples, Ranney advised the conference to be certain of what it intended to accomplish and to obtain "some awareness of possible side effects, because I think you can be sure that whatever new reforms you adopt may not produce all the results you wanted, and they may produce other results that are almost certain to astonish you."

ROBERT TEETER added to the list of caveats concerning change in the system. His recent research in public opinion shows that voters believe the system does produce reasonably good candidates and that the other objections discussed in the conference "are viewed on the part of the voters at least, as more of a nuisance than they are a hindrance to electing a good president." In contrast, our experience with massive change has been unfortunate.

Teeter emphasized that campaigns really are educational. By the end of the primary season, surely by the end of the general campaign, the voters do know more about the candidates' character, personal qualities, principles, and concerns. He said he saw the whole presidential campaign system, through primaries and elections over many years, as a training or preparation period in which candidates acquire seniority on the national scene. John Kennedy, Richard Nixon, Lyndon Johnson, and Ronald Reagan were participants on the national scene for a number of years before each was finally accepted for the presidency. The primaries and caucuses should therefore be viewed as parts of the whole system of developing national candidates whom the people trust and will accept.

NELSON POLSBY stood firm on what came to be called the Polsby doctrine. "I think the best thing this group can do is to admonish the national parties that centralized criteria and centralized solutions ought to be withheld and that state parties ought to be allowed to regain their capacities to send delegates to national party conventions by whatever means they choose. No racial exclusions are permissible. Other than that, all orders from headquarters ought to be regarded as bad for the national parties, for state parties, for the nomination process, for mobilizing voters, and bad for recruiting good candidates." Polsby held that we must have respect for state parties and shun national intrusion. He therefore opposed the Udall plan for limited regional primaries.

The real problem, he said, is that the process centers entirely on the candidate. This weakens the party in the states where it should be strong. "We looked to the national party for reform and it got us in a mess. It is time we trusted the state parties not to perpetuate these problems."

ROBERT FINCH declared, "I will argue today that what we have now in the primary system is a nonsystem." Drawing on his long experience in Los Angeles county, California state, and national Republicn politics, he described past primaries for state office in California, as well as presidential primaries there, as incidental to state intraparty struggles for control and for party unification. Deciding who should be nominated for president was clearly of secondary importance. Instead, control of politics within each California political party was the primary goal. Since the presidential primary of this largest state comes late, long after New Hampshire, it often has little effect. A question of fairness arises here. In today's state caucus, primary, and convention system we have fifty different sets of rules, players, and stakes. "But what can the candidate do when these are the only games in town?"

Finch said nomination and election to national offices, presidential as well as congressional, should be separated from the contests for state and local offices. A uniform federal elections law and ballot that would standardize and govern both primaries and elections to national office is needed rather than patchwork repair. This would ensure voting rights to those who move from one location to another, control the numbers and times of primaries, tie congressional and presidential elections together, and avoid the potential disaster of an electoral college result that contradicts the results of the popular vote for president. He referred to a written account of his proposals that appeared in the *Congressional Record*, April 11, 1972.

Campaign Cost and Finance

David Adamany said, "I do not believe that expenditure limits serve any particular purpose, even if we are not reaching them. I take strong exception, however, to Michael Malbin's suggestion that we do away with the contribution limits." Adamany contended that limits on individual and other contributions to presidential campaigns have reduced the influence wealthy contributors can acquire. "It may be they should be raised, but we do need to remember what the purpose of those contribution limits is."

He recognized that fund-raising operations and operators are important in current presidential politics, but averred that Mark Hanna and other financial operators were there long before the limits were established and will remain with us, regardless of regulations on contributions.

Adamany disagreed with the suggestion that raising money in small amounts lengthens the campaign process. "We heard this morning that what lengthens the campaign is the need for repeated media exposure and desire to have an ongoing spectacle over the years so you can get your name before the voters for the purposes of the primaries."

He advocated reforming the parties. They are strong bureaucratic organizations that run mailing lists and take polls, but not strong associations of political activists with common philosophic goals. That is what they should be, and we should seek to make them so.

Finally, Adamany was troubled by the license current campaign finance laws grant to political action committees (PACs), "not to involve themselves as organized associations, but to use treasury funds, labor union funds, and corporate funds alike, to operate as political action committees. . . ." These aggregations of wealth and political power use acquired capital to influence our egalitarian voting system. Unlike the parties, these organizations are not accountable in our electoral process. The parties need to be strengthened so that they can exert much more influence than do the political action committees.

In his response to Adamany, Michael Malbin said he never advocated eliminating contribution limits, but he could argue for doing so. What he does advocate is raising the limits drastically, perhaps above $100,000, to enable a candidate who needs financial help to get started. Subterfuges were used even in the last nomination race to fund early efforts. At the same time small contributions should be encouraged, and full tax exemption should be made for those who contribute in small amounts. Fund raising is still an important factor in lengthening the campaign effort. Walter Mondale worked on organization and fund raising for two years before he began public campaign activities.

Frank Fahrenkopf summarized his view of the papers and the discussion by concluding that "there does not seem to be any evidence that independent expenditures at this point in time have had a deleterious effect on the presidential primary process." He noted that broadening the discussion to include congressional races and other elections would give greater grounds for criticism of the political actions of these committees.

"The better way to resolve the problems for those who see danger in independent expenditures and political action committees is to take the reins off the two major political parties. They are the broadest amalgams of people of all the political spectrum." Fahrenkopf said his party raised $100 million in the past two years with an average contribution of $35. This was proof that the parties are not just bureaucracies. The parties are the largest combinations of people of different views. If the parties are moved to center stage in the presidential selection process, the problem of interest groups and their large contributions may be reduced if not resolved.

Today the parties are in untenable positions, he said. In 1984 we could not use our regular publications to advocate the reelection of Ronald Reagan. "If we did so, the cost of publication and mailing would have applied against the Reagan-Bush Committee's spending limits. Why were Chuck Manatt and I, as the heads of the official parties who nominate these people, not able to advocate their election without hurting the campaign? Every voting citizen knows that if either party spends a dollar, it is spent to elect the party's candidate."

Fahrenkopf said he favored eliminating public financing, though there are good reasons for and against doing so. If there were no federal financing, he would see no problems for unlimited private personal contribution, "so long as it is disclosed." Since public financing will not be eliminated, however, he would recommend that the $1,000 limit be raised to $5,000. The PAC limit should go to $10,000.

NEIL STAEBLER, drawing upon his years of experience as a Democratic state chairman in Michigan, advocated continued regulation and limitation of financial contributions and warned against forgetting why these limits were originally required. "Disclosure works pretty well, and the information is useful. It is somewhat self-policing and one of the positive advantages of the election act."

He said the ideal way of getting money in politics is to raise it in comparatively small amounts. "When you approach a person for a contribution, you get him thinking about politics. You have a great educational process taking place. Individual contributions are the ideal way to raise money because of all the associated consequences."

Staebler opposed the removal of contribution limitations. "Nothing will undermine overall confidence in the election system more than unlimited contributions," he emphasized.

HERBERT ALEXANDER called attention to the interrelationship of recommendations on finance and contributions to the current prenomination system. A change, such as moving to regional primaries or a national primary, would require a considerable increase in campaign financing. That would be a significant hurdle for candidates who were not front-runners. He expressed specific concern about the proposed elimination of the tax checkoff in the current tax reforms presented by the Reagan administration. He saw that "as an indirect flank attack on the principle of public funding. I do not think we can even go on the assumption there is going to be public funding in 1988 if there is tax simplification with some of the proposals now contained in it."

Upon being questioned by President Ford, Alexander described the distinction between the federal income tax credit for contributions to any recognized political activity and the checkoff, which funds presidential campaigning. Less than 5 percent of those who submit returns take the tax credit, but 25 to 30 percent of the returns call for the one-dollar checkoff each year. This is, however, the source of federal funds for presidential campaigns. Alexander doubted that Congress would replace that fund if its source should be cut off. He said the current annual yield is about $40 million, as it accumulates between presidential election years.

PRESIDENT FORD disagreed with Michael Malbin, who recommended an increase to $60 million for the ceiling on a presidential campaign. He saw that as he saw similar round figures presented to Congress without any justification. He added, "If spending more money will mean that we will have more TV, more mail coming from various organizations asking me and everybody else to contribute more money, I am totally opposed to it."

PUBLIC INVOLVEMENT

Here discussants looked intensively at voters, the various publics including interest groups, the media in the nominating process, and the need to increase voter participation. Developing a widespread awareness of the candidates and a knowledge of their abilities as well as their positions on issues also weighed on the minds of those who spoke.

PHILIP BUCHEN saw the goal of the nomination process as choosing the one candidate who is most likely to win the general election, or the most qualified to become president. Many party leaders sometimes think our present process is the worst way, he recognized, "but to test vote-getting ability, it seems to me the primary is the best opportunity." The exception is when similar candidates divide the vote. "The best known may divide the center vote, and a dark horse could slip in."

For professionals, "the caucus has always been regarded as the better way to evaluate the candidates. It may be that the best solution would be the combination of the caucus and the preference primary, so that you get the two working together.''

Another goal of the nominating process is to help the nominee get elected. ''One thing the party wants is to generate excitement, publicity, and interest. The party that has the dullest primaries because there is no contention probably does its candidates a disservice compared to the party that has very exciting primaries and caucuses.''

Buchen saw possibilities in Martin Wattenberg's proposal for a convention followed by a national primary, but there is need for further clarification, he added.

WILLIAM SCHNEIDER argued that the early presidential primaries are publicity contests. The candidates vie for media attention first of all. ''Do you really believe candidates in New Hampshire are competing for the votes of eighteen out of almost four thousand delegates at the Democratic national convention? That is nonsense. The candidates are competing for publicity.''

In the primaries, the public and the press find a common interest because both are antiestablishment. Voters from both parties exercise their populist tendency by taking on the in group and its favored candidate. This accounts for some of the unanticipated results in the 1984 Democratic primaries. The press, Schneider maintained, is always out to get someone too, so the press rather enjoys the process and takes part in it. Very often this phenomenon encourages ideological activists, and even splinter candidates on the right and on the left. Although Gary Hart and Jimmy Carter were not leftists, ''they were in their respective ways very strongly antiestablishment in their appeal to the primary electorates.'' Schneider saw this as the central problem of the present primary process.

WERNER VEIT questioned the assumption that ''it is useful to have some kind of a general civics class for the electorate that goes on during the long campaign process.'' Some knowledge may be gained about the candidates and their stands, but that knowledge is restricted primarily to people who are already interested. He cited the discouraging number of nonvoters and suggested that the news media, both press and television, are doing absolutely nothing that reaches those people. ''Whatever we are doing, it is not having much effect.''

He then questioned the assumption that media coverage is independent of the political process itself. The media report what they see. ''The reason the media's coverage is so chaotic is that the process is chaotic. The reason no issues are reported is that none surface.''

The presidential primaries are costly events for newspapers. They gain little advertising. Covering the primaries across the continent is expensive, and there is no change in circulation: it does not increase because of presidential primaries or elections. In contrast, if there is a baseball strike, circulation drops noticeably. Before we propose reforms in the way the media cover presidential elections, we need a fundamental change in presidential politics. Apparently, he said, most readers just do not get involved.

MARLIN FITZWATER noted two concepts in the conference. One, the media have taken over the primary election process but are not totally accurate in the presentation of the candidates and the issues. Two, the primary season is too long and getting longer. He asked that the conference reexamine some of the proposals for change already presented. "If we had a primary of two or three months, would that exacerbate the press problem? Would not that in reality cause the media to have an even greater role in determining the outcome?"

DAVID MATHEWS used the findings of Kettering's Public Agenda Foundation as the base for his observations. He posited first "that people who do not know where Guatemala is nonetheless have some substantial contributions to make to political debate." People would accept reform in the presidential selection system if such reform were seen as an improvement. They would not, however, accept any change they saw as advancing party power or the influence of professionals at the expense of the citizens. If the parties, the professionals, and the people were in agreement, reforms would pass muster.

Mathews distinguished between a mass and a public. A public in our democratic system is that group of people who understand their relationship to one another, while a mass of people have no connections or relationship to each other. Democracy depends upon the deliberation of the publics and of their arriving at an agreeable solution. Public attitudes tend to cohere toward a pragmatic middle.

"What I am suggesting is there may be a constituency for reforms, not just in the electoral system but in the general processes of government, and that the public will accept those reforms that tend to, in a very pragmatic way, make the system more sensible, that decrease special interest, and that militate against factionalism."

LANA POLLACK urged that the state parties must be given leeway, otherwise they may not produce or accept candidates for whom the active state party people will work. "We should not reduce parochialism too much. There are problems in all state systems, but we can live with differences between our states." She stressed the need for the federalist element and for giving those who work in state and local activities a voice in selecting the candidate. That is the essential part of fairness and legitimacy, she held.

JACK WALKER introduced the idea of holding primary and general elections on Sundays or holidays. This should increase turnout and also increase acceptance of the primaries and elections as fair and legitimate. The present system has developed because of populistic concerns, yet "people are distrustful of the system, and I think it is very important to establish its legitimacy. It has to be elaborate enough, and long enough, and exhausting enough so that people think it is a fair test."

Group Recommendations

During the last session of the conference, after reviewing the presentations and discussions, each conferee chose to join one of three groups that were charged with formulating recommendations for changing or not changing the prenomination process in three broad areas: (1) "Alternatives to the Present System," chaired by Richard Cheney, U.S. congressman from Wyoming; (2) "Campaign Financing," chaired by David Adamany, president of Wayne State University; and (3) "Voters, Communications, Party, and Interest Groups," chaired by Philip Converse, director of the Center for Political Studies at The University of Michigan. After their deliberations, each group chairman reported his group's recommendations to President Ford. Alexander Heard, chancellor of Vanderbilt University, presided over the final session.

RICHARD CHENEY said his group on alternatives to the present system first considered Tom Mann's four broad approaches: (1) to make no change whatever, (2) to go back to the old system of letting elites choose the presidential candidate, (3) to standardize or to improve the present system through important but marginal changes, or (4) to recommend radical changes, such as establishing a national primary. The group adopted the third approach, that of improving the present system, and eliminated the national primary as part of the radical change alternative. It also shunned any plan to let political elites choose presidential nominees.

The participants considered adjusting the present system so that there would be federal financial sanctions against those candidates who opened their campaigns too early, but that proposal encountered opposition. Instead, some members, including the chairman of the group, took the view that the role of the states in selecting delegates and in the nominating process should be strengthened and unhampered by federal restrictions. The proposition that parties within the states must be strengthened won wide acceptance without opposition.

Cheney noted that the Democratic party's Fairness Commission might soon consider the Udall proposal for regional primaries. Recalling President Ford's warning that the current conference membership included a number of Republicans and so should not be seen as a GOP conclave advising the Democrats, Cheney's group avoided specifics. Instead, its sense was that the nominating process is too long and frustrating. There are questions of legitimacy and the like, ''but the bottom line is it is extremely difficult to come up with specific recommendations to fix it that are not in the end subject to manipulation by those who want to manipulate the process—the candidates themselves. It is extremely difficult to devise a system that ultimately will not be subject to the same kinds of abuses we see now.''

DAVID ADAMANY commented on the paradoxical nature of his group on campaign financing. Its members agreed that current finance laws were too complex, then recommended changes that would increase the complexity. The members recognized the high cost of the prenomination process, then approved recommendations that would permit cost increases.

There was general but not unanimous agreement that the public financing of prenomination campaigns is necessary so long as there are limits on private contributions. The conferees also recommended that contribution limits for individuals should be increased to $2,000 or even as high as $5,000 for a candidate. Since current limits were established more than a decade ago, inflation has taken its toll. Most in the group agreed that contribution limits for PACs should not be raised. Instead, PACs should be required to report ''soft money'' contributions (loans and facilities) as well as contributions in kind (hours used in campaign support). Any new rules or procedures should be designed, however, so that they do not discourage small unions or other organizations from participating and contributing. The need for files and red tape could well discourage participation.

Disclosure has worked well and should be continued. If it is continued, limits on contributions can be raised. Tax credits for political contributions are little used and should be eliminated. The one-dollar checkoff on the income tax return should be continued without any increase.

The group recommended that state-by-state limits on individual candidates' expenditures be eliminated. These are not effective, particularly where small states border each other, and television coverage crosses boundaries. Limits by states should be raised or eliminated, leaving only a national limit. This change might open up the civic education process.

To facilitate the dissemination of campaign finance information and disclosure, the records of the Federal Election Commission should be made immediately available via remote terminals that can be placed in state capitals. This would speed up disclosure.

Some group members pointed to the lack of funds that each candidate experiences toward the end of the preconvention period. They recommended that federal matching funds be parceled out through the campaign period and increased in amount during the later stages of the nomination campaign. There was almost a consensus that large gifts should be allowed as seed money at the start of the prenomination campaign.

142

In sum the group recommended increased flexibility in finance laws, increased campaign spending, and the opportunity for greater yet disclosed private contributions.

PHILIP CONVERSE opened the report for his group on voters, communications, party, and interest groups with several generalizations about the framing of the groups recommendations. They were formulated to regularize the current system and do fine tuning. The proposal for a national primary was not considered as an option. The members saw their role "as commenting from the populist view on representation, on voters and what they need to have and need to know, and what we can expect any kind of prenomination system to provide." The participants searched for improvement in legitimacy and in civic education and for ways to mobilize and to activate voters. Higher turnout was accepted as part of a healthier system. To obtain these the members first made a simple recommendation that primaries be held on days other than working days, as is done in other parts of the world. They recommended, too, that steps be taken to make registration easier in the primary period and to facilitate absentee voting.

Despite Warren Miller's findings from the 1984 primary season, many members were not of the opinion that civic education ended on Super Tuesday. In the group discussion, with Miller participating, members agreed that the prenomination campaign period should not be shortened to the extent his 1984 findings may imply. They sensed that after the front-loading period, after candidates gain recognition, the quality of coverage improves.

"In other words," Converse stated, "I think from the civic education side, we have a feeling that some shortening and some grouping, conceivably into time zone primaries, would be fine, but the truncation of the time element in the national primary does not gain our support." The group saw value in a process that permits and improves voter information and education.

The group was most concerned that any prenomination system be seen by the voter as legitimate. The privacy of voting must be preserved; it apparently was not in at least one state in 1984. Caucuses and primaries may be used in balance if this will strengthen the party leadership and workers while giving the regular voter a say in selection. State parties must be strong, and their elites should believe that their involvement makes a difference.

Converse noted that other recommendations were considered by the group, but were not supported in strength.

ALEXANDER HEARD first entertained general commentary from the floor and then thanked the discussants and their chairmen as he ended the session on reports and recommendations, and thus concluded the business of the conference. He turned the gathering over to President Ford.

PRESIDENT FORD expressed his great appreciation for the preparation and participation each member of the conference contributed, as he brought the conference to a close. He said, "I have never attended a conference that approached such difficult issues, ones charged with emotion and differences of opinion, and yet emerged with such constructive attitudes, views, and comments as this one. For that I thank you, as I thank you all for being here."

Index

(Page numbers in italics designate tables and figures.)

145

Selected AEI Publications

The Presidential Nominating Process: Can It Be Improved? Jeane J. Kirkpatrick, et al. (1980, 27 pp., $3.25)

Dismantling the Parties: Reflections on Party Reform and Party Decomposition, Jeane J. Kirkpatrick (1978, 31 pp., $3.25)

Money and Politics in the United States: Financing Elections in the 1980s, Michael J. Malbin, ed. (1984, 324 pp., $12.95)

Channels of Power: The Impact of Television on American Politics, Austin Ranney (1983, 207 pp., $14.95)

Parties, Interest Groups, and Campaign Finance Laws, Michael J. Malbin, ed. (1980, 384 pp., cloth $15.25, paper $8.25)

Choosing Presidential Candidates: How Good Is the New Way? Ken Bode, et al. (1980, 30 pp., $3.75)

Participation in American Presidential Nominations, 1976, Austin Ranney (1977, 37 pp., $3.25)

The Federalization of Presidential Primaries, Austin Ranney (1978, 40 pp., $3.25)

AEI Associates Program

The American Enterprise Institute invites your participation in the competition of ideas through its AEI Associates Program. This program has two objectives: (1) to extend public familiarity with contemporary issues; and (2) to increase research on these issues and disseminate the results to policy makers, the academic community, journalists, and others who help shape public policies. The areas studied by AEI include Economic Policy, Education Policy, Energy Policy, Fiscal Policy, Government Regulation, Health Policy, International Programs, Legal Policy, National Defense Studies, Political and Social Processes, and Religion, Philosophy, and Public Policy. For the $49 annual fee, Associates receive

- a subscription to *Memorandum,* the newsletter on all AEI activities
- the AEI publications catalog and all supplements
- a 30 percent discount on all AEI books
- a 40 percent discount for certain seminars on key issues
- subscriptions to any two of the following publications: *Public Opinion,* a bimonthly magazine exploring trends and implications of public opinion on social and public policy questions; *Regulation,* a bimonthly journal examining all aspects of government regulation of society; and *AEI Economist,* a monthly newsletter analyzing current economic issues and evaluating future trends (or for all three publications, send an additional $12).

Call 202/862-7170 or write: AMERICAN ENTERPRISE INSTITUTE
1150 Seventeenth Street, N.W., Suite 301, Washington, D.C. 20036